KANT

and

REVOLUTION

Lenval A. Callender

Published 2011 by arima publishing

www.arimapublishing.com

ISBN 978 1 84549 469 8
© Lenval A. Callender 2011

All rights reserved

This book is copyright. Subject to statutory exception and to provisions of relevant collective licensing agreements, no part of this publication may be reproduced, stored in a retrieval system, or transmitted in any form or by any means, without the prior written permission of the author.

Printed and bound in the United Kingdom

Typeset in Garamond 12/16

This book is sold subject to the conditions that it shall not, by way of trade or otherwise, be lent, re-sold, hired out, or otherwise circulated without the publisher's prior consent in any form of binding or cover other than that which it is published and without a similar condition including this condition being imposed on the subsequent purchaser.

The moral rights of the author have been asserted

Swirl is an imprint of arima publishing.

arima publishing
ASK House, Northgate Avenue
Bury St Edmunds, Suffolk IP32 6BB
t: (+44) 01284 700321
www.arimapublishing.com

"Consistency is the highest obligation of a philosopher, and yet the most rarely found. The ancient Greek schools give us more examples of it than we find in our *syncretistic* age, in which a certain shallow and dishonest *system of compromise* of contradictory principles is devised, because it commends itself better to a public which is content to know something of everything and nothing thoroughly, so as to please every party." *Critique of Practical Reason.*

Kant and Revolution is the first in a series of essays which address some of the most controversial aspects of Kant's ethical philosophy and challenge conventional interpretations established in the neokantian literature over the past half century. Further titles include *Kant and Lying* and *Kant and Race*. It is hoped that these essays will contribute towards the clarification of issues whose resolution is vital to an informed and intelligent assessment of Kant's practical philosophy as a whole.

Citations of Kant's works are in square brackets and refer to the standard German edition: *Immanuel Kants Schriften*. Ausgabe der königlich preussischen Akademie der Wissenschaften (Berlin: W. de Gruyter, 1902-). For present purposes some abbreviations have been added for volumes VII and VIII: [VIIA], *Anthropology from a Pragmatic Point of View* (1798); [VIIC], *The Conflict of the Faculties* (1798); [VIIIE], *An Answer to the Question: What is Enlightenment?* (1784); [VIIIH], *Review of Gottlieb Hufeland's Essay on the Principles of Natural Right* (1786); [VIIIT], *On the Common Saying: 'This may be True in Theory but it does not Apply in Practice'* (1793); [VIIIP], *Perpetual Peace* (1795); [VIIIU], *Idea for a Universal History from a Cosmopolitan Point of View* (1784). Kant's correspondence is also given in square brackets, e.g. [596]. The English translations used in this essay will be found in the Bibliography.

Lenval A. Callender,
Hove, 2011

KANT AND REVOLUTION

Introduction

Over the centuries the term 'revolution' has acquired a variety of meanings and it is therefore important to begin an examination of Kant's views on this subject where most other commentaries do not, that is to say, with his own definition of the term. Speaking in *The Metaphysics of Morals* of the aphorism "The best constitution is that in which power belongs not to men but to the laws", he writes: "The attempt to realize this idea should not be made by way of revolution, by a leap, that is, by violent overthrow of an already existing defective constitution (for there would then be an intervening moment in which any rightful condition would be annihilated). But if it is attempted by gradual reform in accordance with firm principles, it can lead to continual approximation to the highest political good, perpetual peace."[VI:355]. In considering this definition of revolution (*eine Revolution*) as the violent overthrow of a constitution two points need to be borne in mind. 'Violence' is the term Kant invariably employs for the unjust or unlawful use of force and is not to be confused with 'coercion', the just or lawful use of force. It should also be noted that Kant treats *eine Revolution* and rebellion (*Rebellion, Aufstand*) as essentially the same phenomenon and so uses these terms inter-changeably. In contrast to *eine Revolution* Kant employs two expressions denoting a non-violent process of constitutional reform both of which happen to include the word 'revolution': "*eine Revolution der Umbildung*", or a reformative revolution[1], is found in his 1784 essay *Idea for a*

Universal History from a Cosmopolitan Point of View, whilst "*eine Revolution des Volks*", or a 'people's revolution', is a concept found in *On the Right of People to Revolution*, a work published in 1795 by the Nuremberg physician and political philosopher J.B. Erhard, one of Kant's correspondents. Like Kant, Erhard maintains that a coherent constitution cannot contain a legal *right* to *eine Revolution* but insists that *eine Revolution des Volks* is nevertheless demanded on moral grounds. He defines revolution in general as "a radical change in the basic constitution of a state" and distinguishes between *eine Revolution* (apparently as in Kant) and *eine Revolution des Volks*, an evolutionary process of constitutional reform. He states that *eine Revolution des Volks* is not a rebellion (*Rebellion*) or an insurrection (*Insurrektion*) but is to be understood as a morally-inspired movement directed towards the establishment of basic human rights, a development he sees as coincident with that self-emancipation of which Kant himself speaks in his 1784 essay *An Answer to the Question: What is Enlightenment?* The accurate use of these various expressions is essential to understanding all of Kant's remarks on revolution in the years 1784-1798, to his views on the lawful and unlawful use of force by a citizen or a state authority, and is also the key to his unconventional interpretation of the events in France in the spring and early summer of 1789[2].

As with his denial of a *legal* right to lie Kant's contention that a coherent system of justice requires the unconditional prohibition of a *legal* right to revolution (*eine Revolution*) is commonly described in the secondary literature as 'notorious' and 'infamous' and frequently cited as one of the clearest examples of what is said to be the rigoristic, inflexible and even inhuman character of aspects of his moral and political philosophy. Often associated with views of this kind is the charge of incoherence, and indeed a survey of the scholarly literature might lead one to conclude that far from being the systematic thinker he sets out to be the architect of the Critical Philosophy is on this particular issue the author of arguments that at best are confused and perplexing and at worst patently contradictory. The following remark from Ladd (1999: xxxix) is typical: "Admittedly, at times he does seem to adopt extreme positions that appear to be incompatible with one another. The most noteworthy instance of this is his view concerning the French Revolution; he eulogizes this important event of his times as a "moral cause" inserting itself into history while (even on the same page) condemning revolution as something that is always "unjust" "[3]. The work in question is the second Part of *The Conflict of the Faculties* (1798), *An Old Question Raised Again: Is the Human Race Constantly Progressing?* and there is no doubt that here Kant does speak with approval of "the revolution of a gifted people" [VIIC:§7] and he does condemn 'revolution' as at all times unjust; and of course if Kant is using the *word* 'revolution' here in exactly the same sense then he is surely guilty of a blatant contradiction. Yet in *The Conflict of the Faculties* Kant makes it clear enough that in the case of France he is referring to Erhard's concept of *eine Revolution des Volks*, an occurrence which, he says, is a phenomenon "...not of revolution, but (as Erhard puts it) a phenomenon of the *evolution* of a constitution governed by *natural right*. Such a constitution cannot itself be achieved by furious struggles – for civil and foreign wars will destroy whatever *statutory* order has hitherto prevailed – but it does lead us to strive for a constitution which would be incapable of bellicosity, i.e. a republican one." [VIIC: §7] The essential difference between *eine Revolution* and *eine Revolution des Volks*, consistently overlooked in the scholarly literature for more than two centuries, is discussed in both Parts of this essay.

In addition to this charge of inconsistency, the 'paradox' to which Beck (1971), Korsgaard (2000) and so many others refer, is the damning indictment that Kant's denial of a legal right to revolution deprives the citizen of the use of force in resisting the abuses of a tyrannical ruling power and requires that he do no more than passively disobey or meekly submit to whatever is demanded of him. This picture of Kant's hapless citizen is painted by Beck in his influential paper of 1971: "We are not, therefore, justified in killing a tyrant in order to preserve the lives of thousands or millions of his subjects. The most I can morally do is to expose the abuses of his power and make proposals for reform, to disobey him if he commands me to do something immoral and to suffer martyrdom if necessary." This interpretation is reinforced in a paper by Nicholson, *Kant on the Duty Never to Resist the Sovereign* (1976) in which it is said that Kant fails to distinguish between revolution, rebellion and resistance.[5] Reiss (1991) agrees and remarks: "Kant's rejection of the right of resistance, rebellion, or revolution (he uses all these three terms without distinction) under all circumstances, on the one hand, and his enthusiasm for the constitutional aims of the French revolutionaries, on the other, appear at first sight to be paradoxical. Indeed, his rejection of revolution seems incompatible with his own basic principles of politics." Sullivan (1994:25) makes the same claim: "Kant argued that there can be no right to forceful civil resistance to unjust laws.." Similar views can be found in a multitude of other works including *Kant: The Philosophy of Right* (Murphy, 1970), *Kant's Political Philosophy* (Williams, 1983), *Kant's Theory of Justice* (Rosen, 1993), *Creating the Kingdom of Ends* (Korsgaard, 1996), *Respect, Pluralism and Justice* (Thomas E. Hill, 2000), and *Kant's Critique of Hobbes* (Williams, 2003).

According to the conventional wisdom then there is a serious gap in Kant's political philosophy. Nevertheless Schwarz (1977) who appears to be the lone voice of dissent believes there is something deeply amiss in the traditional interpretation and although he does not provide a convincing refutation he is surely correct when he asks: "What interest could a moral philosophy hold for us that delivers man, without recourse, to the powers of the state?" So could the philosopher portrayed by Beck *et al* really be the same one who, speaking "On Servility" in *The Metaphysics of Morals* in 1797, urges every citizen: "Be no man's lackey. Do not let others trample with impunity on your rights." [VI: 436]? Or the same one who writes in *The Conflict of the Faculties* in 1798: "Why has a ruler never dared openly to declare that he recognizes absolutely no right of the people opposed to him, that his people owe their happiness solely to the beneficence of a government which confers this happiness upon them, and that all presumption of the subject to a right opposed to a government (since this right comprehends the concept of permissible resistance), is absurd and even culpable? The reason is that such a public declaration would rouse all of his subjects against him.." [VIIC: §6]. Referring to what he takes Kant's view of resistance to be Nicholson writes: "…one might argue that one has a right to resist the sovereign because of the inalienable right to resist any man who threatens one's life…" and goes on to maintain that Kant does not adopt this approach. But if there are gaps in Kant's ethical system one can safely say that this is not one of them for like everyone else Nicholson takes no account of Kant's use of *ius inculpatae tutelae*, the "right to blameless self-defence" [VI: 235]. According to Kant this inalienable right entitles a citizen to the lawful employment of lethal force in resisting a murderous assault and of course a right of this kind is not at all the same as a right to *eine Revolution*. This fatal omission thus lends support to the view of so many political philosophers that a citizen confronted with state violence is reduced to adopting one of only two alternatives, either *eine Revolution* or slavish submission; and since the latter is so clearly at odds with even the vaguest notions of human dignity most opt for the former. But neither alternative can be honestly defended on the basis of Kant's published works and, once again, the strategy he does advocate does not appear in the secondary literature.

By 1785 Kant had formulated two principles which he claims place determinate and strict limits on the *just* exercise of sovereign and executive power and both are said to be derived *a priori*; the first sanctions only passive resistance but the second permits the active use of force. The first of these principles is stated in 1784 in *An Answer to the Question: What is Enlightenment?* in which Kant writes: "The touchstone of whatever can be decided upon as law for people lies in the question: whether people could impose such a law upon itself." [VIIIE: 39]. This important principle is found in all of Kant's later works on political philosophy and is directly related to his concept of sovereignty: since on this view a sovereign power is said to represent the united collective will of a people it is not *justly* entitled to impose any legislation which a people could not impose upon itself. In *Theory and Practice* nine years later he writes of this "infallible *a priori* standard" - the idea of an "original contract" - as follows: "For so long as it is not self-contradictory to say that an entire people could agree to such a law, however painful it might seem, then the law is in harmony with right. But if a public law is beyond reproach (i.e. *irreprehensible*) with respect to right, it carries with it the authority to coerce those to whom it applies, and conversely, it forbids them to resist the will of the legislator by violent means. In other words, the power of the state to put the law into effect is also *irresistible*, and no rightfully established commonwealth can exist without a force of this kind to suppress all internal resistance. For such resistance would be dictated by a maxim which, if it became general, would destroy the whole civil constitution and put an end to the only state in which men can possess rights." [VIIIT: 299]. In essence this principle requires that like cases be treated alike but so far as resistance to the will of the state is concerned it should be noted that Kant does not condemn resistance *per se* but specifically resistance conducted by "*violent means*".

Kant's second principle limiting the just exercise of sovereign and executive power was advanced one year later in the *Groundwork of the Metaphysics of Morals* – it is the categorical imperative – and this ethical principle plays a far greater role in Kant's political philosophy than the secondary literature would lead one to suppose. In fact its role is pivotal, as can be seen in the following remark from Kant in 1797: "…why is the doctrine of morals usually called (especially by Cicero) a doctrine of *duties* and not also a doctrine of *rights*, even though rights have reference to duties? – The reason is that we know our own freedom (from which all moral laws, and so all rights as well as duties proceed) only through the *moral imperative*, which is a proposition commanding duty, from which the capacity for putting others under obligation, that is, the concept of right, can afterwards be explicated." [VI: 239]. Thus in Kant's practical philosophy all rights derive ultimately from the categorical imperative and so include those referred to as *inalienable* in *Against Hobbes* in his *Theory and Practice* of 1793. It should also be carefully noted that it is the universal law formulation (FUL) of this imperative that also determines the *legality* (as distinct from the *morality*) of an action and so forms the basic "principle of right" to which Kant refers in his *Perpetual Peace* of 1795: "Act in such a way that you can will your maxim to become a universal law (irrespective of what the end in view may be)" [VIIIP: 377].

So if a person has *inalienable* rights, rights which as such must obtain even in a hypothetical pre-civil condition, how could it possibly arise that a citizen has a legal or moral duty to passively submit to whatever another decides to inflict upon him whether this be an individual or some state authority? This is not the position stated by Kant in the *Rechtslehre*: "*Obey the authority that has*

power over you (in whatever does not conflict with inner morality)…"
[VI: 371]. This statement is usually regarded as rather innocuous but when it is realised that it is from this 'inner morality' that Kant also claims to establish the innate and inalienable rights of a citizen then its true political significance begins to become apparent. For if it were really Kant's view that a citizen has an unqualified duty to obey then the inalienable rights he defends in *Against Hobbes* and elsewhere would be devoid of practical meaning since a legal right one could be legally bound not to exercise is a patent absurdity and can be no right at all. But even had Kant not defended the idea of inalienable rights it is surely fallacious to conclude from the proposition that a citizen is not entitled to employ force in an attempt to overthrow a constitution that he is not entitled to employ force for any purpose at all. Kant does not provide specific deductions for this or that inalienable right but as described in Part I of this essay if one follows the method he outlines it is not difficult to demonstrate how a right such as *ius inculpatae tutelae* can be derived from FUL.

A further issue concerns the interpretation of Kant's remarks on what he sometimes calls "an event of our time" but which everyone else always calls 'The French Revolution'. Although Kant was not the first to challenge traditional views of this event he was certainly not the last and in 1954 Cobban, Professor of French History at University College London, created something of a stir with his inaugural lecture entitled *"The Myth of the French Revolution"*. The particular myth which concerned Cobban was the belief that The French Revolution was organised and led by representatives of a progressive bourgeoisie whose aim was the destruction of feudalism and the introduction of full-scale capitalism, a belief underpinning the view described by the French historian Furet as the "Jacobino-Marxist Vulgate". Cobban relates how he had considered an even more provocative title, *"Was there a French Revolution?"*, but decided against it in order not to offend the sensibilities of the French ambassador who would be present. But had Cobban's original question been put the answer would have to depend upon exactly what one means by 'revolution' and in *The Metaphysics of Morals* Kant takes issue with what he sees as another myth, namely, that the transfer of legislative and sovereign power from the absolute monarchy to the National Assembly in the critical period *between* May 5th and July 14th 1789 – that is, up to but *not* including the assault on the Bastille - was actually brought about by a successful attempt to violently overthrow the existing monarchical constitution. He writes: "A powerful ruler in our time therefore made a very serious error in judgement when, to extricate himself from the embarrassment of large state debts, he left it to the people to take this burden on itself and distribute it as it saw fit; for then the legislative authority naturally came into the people's hands, not only with regard to the taxation of subjects but also with regard to the government, namely to prevent it from incurring new debts by extravagance and war. The consequence was that the monarch's sovereignty wholly disappeared (it was not merely suspended) and passed to the people, to whose legislative will the belongings of every subject became subjected." [VI: 341].

This interpretation is based upon Erhard's concept of *eine Revolution des Volks* and Kant seems to think it obvious that anyone familiar with France during that period would arrive at the same conclusion. Critics of his interpretation do not distinguish between his different uses of the word 'revolution' and usually confine themselves to a few perfunctory remarks rather than a detailed examination of the course of events in France at that time. Like so many others it seems that neo-kantian political philosophers have been seduced by the miraculous quality of that phrase, 'The French Revolution', which by the accumulated weight of entrenched conviction has the power to transform even the slightest act of defiance into an attempt to overthrow a constitution by force. Some even seem to believe that from a constitutional point of view the key political event actually occurred on July 14th. Williams (1983:211) describes Kant's interpretation as "highly idiosyncratic" whilst Beck thinks it both paradoxical and a "sophistic legalism". Beck maintains that if the transfer of legislative and sovereign powers to the National Assembly is not to be regarded as a revolution (*eine Revolution*) then the attempt to restore Bourbon absolutism by force of arms could not be described as counter-revolutionary as of course it usually is; or to put it another way, on Kant's interpretation Louis XVIth and his supporters in and outside of France would now have to be regarded as the true 'revolutionaries'. It must be admitted that on Kant's interpretation this conclusion is unavoidable but it is one that can appear paradoxical only to those who cannot get beyond the idea that the advocate of *eine Revolution* is bound to be a progressively-minded fighter in the cause of social justice. Yet there is no shortage of examples where a constitution has been violently overthrown by those one might well describe as 'reactionary revolutionaries' and Spain in the years 1936-9 is a case in point. It has only to be recalled that here the elected Popular Front government of the second Republic was violently overthrown by Franco with military support from Nazi Germany and Fascist Italy to appreciate that there is no necessary connection between *eine Revolution* in Kant's sense of this term and anything that could reasonably be called a progressive social development. Had Beck taken account of the different uses Kant makes of the word 'revolution' he would also have realised that the opposing term 'counter-revolution' would now have to be understood in a different way. The conversion of an absolute into a constitutional monarchy is certainly (as Erhard puts it) "a radical change in the constitution of a state" and if this should occur without the use of force Kant would treat it as *eine Revolution des Volks* but otherwise as *eine Revolution*. So in this terminology the reversal of such a process, which of course is also a radical change in the constitution of a state, would have to be regarded as a counter-revolution whatever the means by which it was effected. Thus the forcible conversion of a constitutional into an absolute monarchy would now have to be regarded from one point of view as a counter-revolution but from another as *eine Revolution*.

The most pertinent comments on Kant's view of The French Revolution come from Reiss (1991) although his judgement tends to be clouded by his failure to differentiate between Kant's uses of the word 'revolution' and by his belief that Kant opposes all forceful resistance to constitutional authority . In the 1970 edition of this work Reiss says that Kant's interpretation is "dubious" although he does quote Cobban's *History of Modern France* (1962) as follows: "The calling of the States-General was undoubtedly the critical step, for it meant the abdication of absolute monarchy".

However in a Postscript to the 1991 edition of his own work Reiss remarks: "By convoking the States-General, Louis XVI went further than initiating reforms, according to Kant (though this was not what the king had in mind). He in fact handed over sovereignty to the States General. Thus, from a strictly constitutional point of view, no revolution at all took place in France. As I have suggested, this interpretation of the events in France may, at first sight, appear to be an exercise in casuistry, or at best an excessively legalistic and hence unrealistic interpretation. But this is not in fact the case. It is now widely accepted that the absolute monarchy had come to an end when the king, in order to solve the financial crisis, summoned the States General to Versailles and thereby forfeited sovereignty." In support of this interpretation Reiss refers to Doyle's *Origin of the French Revolution* (1988) in which it is said that to convoke the Estates General in early 1789 was "as much as to announce that power had passed from the king's hands". Doyle makes the same point in his *Oxford History of the French Revolution* (1989) and again in the 2002 edition of the same work.

Despite some truth in his remarks Reiss fails to address the decisive point at issue because he does not detect the essential difference between *eine Revolution* and *eine Revolution des Volks*. For the principal question here is not the transfer of legislative and sovereign power to the National Assembly – for that can hardly be doubted - but rather the *manner* in which this transfer took place; was it the result of a successful attempt to overthrow by force the existing constitution or was it not? And if it was not then Kant is correct in maintaining that what really happened in the early months of 1789 was not *eine Revolution* but rather *eine Revolution des Volks*, that is, "the *evolution* of a constitution governed by *natural right*." If this is so then on his argument one is bound to conclude that the threat to reverse this development by force of arms, a threat to which the assault on the Bastille on 14th July was for the most part a defensive reaction, is to be regarded as an unsuccessful attempt to bring about *eine Revolution*. As described in Part II of this essay a detailed examination of the events at Versailles and Paris in the early months of 1789 lends powerful support to Kant's interpretation.

It would be a mistake to assume that the constitutional development to which Kant refers implies the absence of political conflict and one might even argue as he does in *Perpetual Peace* that conflict is presupposed in the conception of an evolutionary progression towards a genuine republican constitution or at least towards a system that functions in a republican manner. One has to say 'genuine' here since Kant had no illusions about regimes which describe themselves as republics but which like the slave-based state of Rome before Augustus are devoid of the essential features of "natural right". According to Kant this qualification applies not only to the states of antiquity and indeed he describes Cromwell's regime as "an abortive monster of a despotic republic"

[VIIC: §10]. Although he does not refer to the later French Republic in this way it would not have been an inappropriate description for the kind of state which existed in that country when *Theory and Practice* was published in 1793. It would also be a mistake to conclude that his interpretation of the transfer of sovereignty in France is invalidated by events subsequent to it and in his *Anthropology From a Pragmatic Point of View* (1798) he describes the rule of the Committee of Public Safety, formed in the spring of 1793 and soon to come under the influence of Robespierre, as a time "when public injustice is established and declared lawful." [VIIA: 259].

Related to the question of constitutional change in France is the issue of Kant's general attitude towards these events. For reasons discussed elsewhere in this essay many rumours about his opinions circulated at the time and some are related by Gooch in *Germany and the French Revolution* (1920), a work which remains the most extended treatment by an historian of Kant's views on the subject. A number of philosophical accounts begin by carelessly repeating rumours found in this work, particularly those claiming that Kant was sympathetic to Jacobinism. This is a charge he was to deny in no uncertain terms as the work of "slanderous sycophants" [VIIC: §6], and what is so misleading about these modern accounts is that they pay no regard to important changes in the political character of Jacobinism between 1789 and 1791. After all, early members of the Jacobin Club in Paris included not only Robespierre, but clerics like the Abbé Sieyès, a large number of constitutional monarchists including the Comte de Mirabeau and the Marquis de Lafayette, other members of the nobility such as the duc d'Aiguillon, not to mention Louis Phillipe, duc de Chartes, a future king of France. In *Kant On History* (1963: xii) Beck speaks of Kant's "esteem for the French Revolution which remained constant even when most of the earlier partisans of it in Germany had fallen away and left him almost the last and certainly the greatest of the "Jacobins" in Germany", and Korsgaard (1996:31/2), who like Beck relies on Gooch, writes of Kant: "..his enthusiasm for the Revolution was not as idealizing as that of many of its admirers, and he did not turn against it when so many others did. According to one report "he said all the horrors in France were unimportant compared with the chronic evil of despotism from which France had suffered and the Jacobins were probably right in all they were doing." Given the high value he places on freedom and human rights, it is not surprising that he regards a republic as the ideal form of government. But it is surprising to find this enthusiasm for its ruthless establishment in a man who believed that we must always act as citizens in the Kingdom of Ends regardless of consequences, and have faith in God to set things right."

Korsgaard's remark about Jacobins[4], supposed to have been made by Kant in 1794, not only ignores his emphatic public denial but takes no account of established historical fact. The fate of the Jacobin Club in Paris is well-known, at least to historians. The political complexion of this Club changed radically after the flight of the royal family towards the Austrian frontier in June 1791 when most of its members left in protest against a petition declaring that the king had abdicated and should not be re-instated without the support of a national majority. Those deputies who left joined the rival Feuillant Club, the main political influence in the National Constituent Assembly which drafted the constitution of 1791, and when this was (reluctantly) accepted by the king he was formally reinstated as a constitutional monarch. Robespierre remained with the rump of the Club and when it revived it did so in alliance with those sections of the population in Paris and the provinces which had little or no regard for elementary principles of justice. Thus to subscribe to 'Jacobinism' after 1791 was to identify with policies that were to culminate in The Terror of 1793-4 and it was doubtless because of these developments that Kant issued his public denial. Speaking in *The Conflict of the Faculties* of those who were simply advocating a non-violent progression towards a republican form of government he writes : "Nevertheless, some slanderous sycophants, to make themselves important, have sought to pass off this innocuous political twaddle as a fondness for innovation, Jacobinism and mob action which would threaten the state; yet, under the circumstances, there was not even the least reason for these allegations, particularly in a country more than a hundred miles from the scene of the revolution." [VIIC: §6]. Remarks of this kind did not protect Kant from prying in Prussia or his books from bonfires in Bavaria.

Despite his repeated statements to the contrary many commentators claim that there is in Kant's works evidence to suggest that he approves of *eine Revolution*. This seems to arise partly from the widespread assumption that his denial of a legal right to *eine Revolution* must also imply a denial of a citizen's legal right to resist by force the violent acts of a state and partly from a general misunderstanding of his remarks about "the revolution of a gifted people" in France. Since in the latter case no distinction is recognised between *eine Revolution* and *eine Revolution des Volks* the motivations attributed both to the participants and to spectators like Kant are bound to be mistaken. As noted above, Ladd writes that Kant's "eulogizes" the French revolution; Beck speaks repeatedly of "Kant's enthusiasm for the French Revolution"; Korsgaard (1996: 31) that "Kant was an ardent champion of the American and French revolutions", and Williams (2003: 25/6): "…Kant was to retain an enthusiasm for the events in France throughout the rest of his life, but this enthusiasm was tempered by many reservations about the course that politics in fact took in France." Yet in this context Kant never speaks of enthusiasm without specifying what he means and the enthusiasm to which he refers is not for this or that event as such but always "enthusiasm for asserting the rights of man" [VIIC: §6] or "enthusiasm for upholding justice for the human race". As he puts it in *The Conflict of the Faculties*: "…genuine enthusiasm always moves only toward what is ideal and, indeed, to what is purely moral, such as the concept of right". It follows, then, that only insofar as the events in France were movements towards a condition of justice and the practical recognition of basic human rights can they be said to receive any support from Kant's practical philosophy. It is not the case that Kant retained his enthusiasm for the events in France throughout his life for he had no enthusiasm at all for revolution in the sense in which Williams understands Kant's use of this term – that is, as *eine Revolution* - and what he retained throughout his life was an enthusiasm for the rights of Man and that is a different matter altogether.

The moral enthusiasm of which Kant speaks is not to be confused with the sentiments expressed by those neo-kantian writers who still warm to the image of 'the revolutionary' as some kind of romantic hero. In "When the Virtuous Person Revolts", and "Why We Find Revolution Thrilling", Korsgaard (2008:254/262) presents the advocate of *eine Revolution* in a way that would not be out of place in the ethical vacuum of Sartrian Existentialism. The people's revolutionaries of Kant and the observers of whom he is *also* speaking in *The Conflict of the Faculties* at least have that "common rational knowledge of morality" referred to in the *Groundwork of the Metaphysic of Morals*, that is to say, a basic grasp of the moral law (which Korsgaard calls "the universalization test") and of elementary principles of justice. Of the people's revolutionaries themselves Kant remarks: "...Monetary rewards will not elevate the adversaries of the revolution to the zeal and grandeur of soul which the pure concept of right produced in them.."[5] [VIIC: §6], but this distinctly moral motive plays no discernible role in Korsgaard's own conception of 'the revolutionary', an individual who appears to be without ethical guidance of any kind: "It is," she avers, "as if a kind of gap opens up in the moral world in which the moral agent must stand alone..The moment of revolution is a vindication of morality, and so of our humanity. We are masters of our own self-mastery; in control of our self-control. Being human is not sapping our strength, for we still know when to fight. The revolutionary does not *become* strong and free when he picks up his gun. Instead, he proves to us he's been free all along." Such extravagant flights of fancy form no part of authentic Kantian practical philosophy.

This essay is in two Parts: *Inalienable Rights and Revolution* and *France: Notes on Constitutional Change in 1789*. The *Notes* add nothing new to the existing stock of historical information but by drawing attention to some of the less publicised aspects of the constitutional change in May and June of 1789 they offer an interpretation far closer to Kant's *eine Revolution des Volks* than to the traditional *eine Revolution*.

Notes to the Introduction

1. This is Beck's 1971 translation of *eine Revolution der Umbildung*.

2. Since it has been claimed in Germany and France that Erhard was actually an advocate of *eine Revolution* it may be asked whether in *The Conflict of the Faculties* Kant himself accurately expresses Erhard's own view. So far as the present essay is concerned this is not relevant since it is Kant's views on revolution that are under discussion and not Erhard's; Kant understands Erhard to be arguing for a process of reform rather than the violent overthrow of a constitution and that is the main point at issue here. Nevertheless, since Erhard's view has been counter-posed to Kant's it may be helpful to add something more on what Erhard himself seems to mean by his concept of *eine Revolution des Volks*. This is somewhat problematical for even those who see Erhard as an advocate of *eine Revolution* acknowledge that *Über das Recht des Volks zu einer Revolution* contains a number of ambiguities and obscure expressions, deficiencies that are said to be explained by the author's attempt to avoid the attentions of the Censor. This is the view of Gilli (1999), who claims that Erhard departs radically from Kant on 'revolution': *JB Erhard et Le droit du peuple à la Révolution (1795). Entre Kant, Fichte et Rousseau.* Annales Historiques de la Révolution française, No. 317, 477-493. In fact Erhard's book, written in 1794 in the declining phase of The Terror in France, makes only one passing reference to the events in that country ("The French are now a free people but slavish citizens"), and he dismisses 'Jacobins', 'Aristocrats', 'Democrats' and

'Moderantists' as factions unrepresentative of 'the People' as a whole. But serious problems emerge when Erhard attempts to explain the way in which *eine Revolution des Volks* is supposed to occur. Thus whilst he speaks repeatedly of the 'altering' (*Änderung*) of a constitution he also remarks at one point that if a constitution contains a provision which hinders enlightenment the people are entitled to abolish it ("*die Konstitution aufzuheben*"). But 'abolish' what? – the entire constitution or only some particular provision? And how exactly is this 'abolition' to occur? His standpoint on the use of force is also decidedly equivocal. Having sought to distinguish *eine Revolution des Volks* from *eine Revolution* and also from rebellion and insurrection he writes in his conclusion: "In a revolution of the people (*eine Revolution des Volks*) let it not be otherwise thought than that the people sought by force (*Gewalt*) to show its commitment to intervene on the side of the rights of maturity and responsibility and to elevate the legal relationship between itself and the rulers." What is to be understood by Erhard's *Gewalt*? Could it be taken to mean, as a recent French translation has it, "violence"?* He continues: "The concept of a revolution which we gave above was that it is a radical change in the basic constitution of a state; but it can only be more closely defined by reference to the contribution of the originators of the revolution, so the alteration of the constitution must be undertaken for the benefit of the revolutionaries, and a revolution of the people can have no other purpose than to alter the basic constitution in favour of the people. Here we must distinguish between a revolution of the people (*eine Revolution des Volks*) and a revolution (*eine Revolution*), which can only be carried out by the people. In the latter case the people can revolt out of ignorance or delusion, even to its own disadvantage, but one cannot then also say: the people began a revolution, but only: the people allowed itself to be used for revolutionary purposes." Ambiguities of this kind together with his campaign for a republic in southern Germany produced very different contemporary assessments of Erhard and his book. Kant takes *eine Revolution des Volks* to mean the *re-forming* of a constitution by non-violent means and this view is also put forward in a work on state administration by the Austrian J. von Sonnenfels. He writes of Erhard: "He is far from being a revolutionary. There is nothing in his "Rights of Revolution" that is dangerous except its title"**. On the other hand members of the 'Hanoverian Whigs', the conservative circle in Göttingen which took Burke's *Reflections on the Revolution in France* as its oracle denounced Erhard as a dangerous agitator and a threat to the state and his book was banned in Saxony, Bavaria and Austria. However, since Erhard was in direct contact with Kant throughout this period, outlived him by more than twenty years and published several other works after 1795 he had ample opportunity to differentiate his own use of *eine Revolution* from Kant's and if he wished to dissociate himself from the reformist view attributed to him in *The Conflict of the Faculties*. It seems he did neither. In later works he does not challenge Kant's understanding of *eine Revolution des Volks* or dispute Kant's opposition to *eine Revolution* and this is also true of his letters to Kant on 15th November 1795 [688], 16th January 1797 [735], and 16th April 1800 [860], the last written two years after publication of *The Conflict of the Faculties*.

*J.B Erhard, *Du Droit du peuple à faire la revolution et autres ecrits de philosophe politiques (1793-1795)*. Editions l'Age d'Hommes, Lausanne, 1993.

**Sonnenfels, J., *Handbuch der inneren Staatsverwaltung*, Vol.1, Vienna (1798), Preface, XXV.

3. This is a somewhat tempered version of his provocative remark in the 1965 edition of the same work: "The most notorious instance of this is his view concerning the French Revolution; he eulogizes this important event of his times as a "moral cause" inserting itself into history while (even on the same page!) condemning revolution as something that is always "unjust." "

4. Korsgaard cites Gooch as the source of this remark which Gooch himself attributes to Nicolovius, the publisher of several of Kant's works. In a later edition of *Germany and the French Revolution* (1927: 264 & 269) Gooch gives as his source Hettner's *Geschichte der Deutschen Literatur im XVIII. Jahrhundert* of 1856-70 but does not provide a full reference. In a 1928 edition of Hettner's work published in Leipzig the relevant passage occurs in IV, 25; there Hettner cites the biographer K.A. Varnhagen who says he heard it from Stägemann in 1817 who in turn says he was told this by Nicolovius who says that Kant said it in 1794. This does not mean that Nicolovius did not say what he is reported as saying but it does mean that unauthenticated remarks of this kind should have no place in the academic literature. If Nicolovius did make the remark in question it does not prove that he accurately expressed Kant's

view and even Biester, editor of the *Berliner Monatsschrift*, had no idea of Kant's real views on France until he received the manuscript of *Theory and Practice* in 1793. On October 5th of that year Biester writes to Kant: "To speak quite openly, it pleased me all the more since it refuted the rumour (which I suspected from the start) that you had come out in favour of the ever increasingly repulsive French Revolution, in which the actual freedom of reason and morality and all wisdom in statecraft and legislation are being most shamelessly trampled under foot – a revolution that even shatters and annuls the universal principles of constitutional law and the concept of a civil constitution, as I now learn from your essay. Surely it easier to decapitate people (especially if one lets others do it) than courageously to discuss the rational and legal grounds of opposition with a despot, be he sultan or despotic rabble. Till now, however, I see only that the French have mastered those easier operations, performed with bloody hands; I do not see that they have the power of rational examination." [596]. There is no reason to suppose that Nicolovius had any more insight into Kant's views on France than Biester, nor should it be forgotten that 1794, the year Nicolovius is supposed to be speaking of, was at the height of The Terror and if ever there was a year when Kant was less likely to have spoken with approval of the Jacobins it was surely that year. The burden of proof here lies with those who claim otherwise, and if that claim cannot be properly substantiated then Kant is fully justified in calling it a slander.

5. In his attempt to solve 'the paradox' Nicholson (1976) writes: "When, in his discussion of "whether the human race is continually

improving," he invokes the French Revolution as an actual instance of men's goodness and their power to be the authors of their own improvement, he appeals to what is happening *outside* France, to the unselfish sympathy aroused by two political ideals, that a people should be left free by other states to choose its constitution, and that the only just constitution is a "republic." He writes as a spectator, addressing other spectators." The basic problem here is that Nicholson fails to differentiate between *eine Revolution* and *eine Revolution des Volks* and so he seeks a way around Kant's references to moral enthusiasm by trying to avoid the indubitable fact that Kant is speaking here of a kind of revolution he actually supports. So Nicholson attempts to restrict Kant's "moral enthusiasm" to the spectators *outside* of France but as Kant himself writes this enthusiasm for "the pure concept of right" applies just as much to the active participants *inside* of that country as to observers outside. In *Immanuel Kant's Moral Theory* (1989:370) Sullivan adopts the same questionable tactic and for the same reason: "Rather than being an embarrassment to Kant's theory of history, then, for the transcendental *spectator* viewing events and the human race as a collective whole, the French Revolution showed that moral progress can result from immoral conduct." (the emphasis is Sullivan's). To look for consistency in Kant's works is the proper approach but this is inventing it when a careful reading of the original texts would have revealed no inconsistency to begin with.

PART I

INALIENABLE RIGHTS AND REVOLUTION

Before examining Kant's remarks on revolution in the years 1784-1798 it will be useful to explain in more detail his conception of inalienable rights and especially the key right to blameless self-defence. In *Against Hobbes*, the second part of *Theory and Practice*, he states that people "...have inalienable rights against the head of state, even if these cannot be rights of coercion. Hobbes is of the opposite opinion. According to him (*De Cive*, Chap. 7, §14) the head of state has no contractual obligations towards the people; he can do no injustice to a citizen, but may act towards him as he pleases. This proposition would be perfectly correct if injustice were taken to mean any injury which gave the injured party a *coercive* right against the one who has done him injustice. But in its general form, the proposition is quite terrifying..." Later in the same work he writes: "...everyone has his inalienable rights, which he cannot give up even if he wishes to..."; he re-iterates his belief in "...the basic rights of man", and repeats one of the principles said to circumscribe the just limits of sovereign and executive authority: "...the universal principle by which a people has to appraise its rights negatively – that is, appraise merely what may be regarded as not ordained by the supreme legislation, as with its best will – is contained in the proposition: What a people cannot decree for itself, a legislator also cannot decree for a people." [VIIIT: 304].

As mentioned earlier in *Theory and Practice* Kant does not elaborate on these "basic rights of man" and even in *The Metaphysics of Morals* published four years later there is little direct mention of the subject. In the latter work however he refers specifically to a "right to blameless self-defence" and here and elsewhere does indicate the procedure required to derive this right from the categorical imperative. In the course of rejecting the notion of a 'right of necessity' he writes: "This alleged right is supposed to be an authorization to take the life of another who is doing nothing to harm me, when I am in danger of losing my own life. It is evident that were there such a right the doctrine of right would have to be in contradiction with itself. For the issue here is not that of a *wrongful* assailant upon my life whom I forestall by depriving him of his life (*ius inculpatae tutelae*), in which a recommendation to show moderation (*moderanum*) belongs not to right but to ethics. It is instead a matter of violence being permitted against someone who has used no violence against me." [VI: 235]. Although Kant does not draw attention to the fact it is unlikely that he was unaware that the law of *ius inculpatae tutelae* entitled the *blameless* Roman citizen to exercise force in defence of his person and property not only against other members of the public but in some cases even against *unlawful* assault by soldiers, government officials and their agents[1]. Needless to say, everything here turns upon the question of what is to be regarded as lawful and that brings one to Kant's view of the origin and nature of innate rights.

Although the language of 'innate', inalienable' and 'inviolable' rights was common currency by the 18th century there were very different views about their origin and justification. To regard these rights as endowed by a Creator or to merely assert them as self-evident truths is not Kant's way of going about things and the striking feature of his approach is that the inalienable rights he defends are held to arise directly from the fundamental epistemological principles of his ethical philosophy. This is not so with Locke, for example, whose *Treatises of Civil Government* seeking to justify the 'Glorious Revolution' employ ideas whose very possibility is flatly denied by the empiricist epistemological assumptions of his *Essay Concerning Human Understanding* published in the same year. As FitzJames Stephens pointed out many years ago: "The great singularity of the political theory of Locke is its striking incongruity with his metaphysics. The object of the Essay on the Human Understanding is to destroy the doctrine of innate ideas, and to reduce all knowledge to a generalisation of experience. Its moral side consisted principally in the reduction of morality to a system of criminal law with supernatural sanctions. The Treatise on Civil Government appears, as the previous outline of its principal doctrines sufficiently proves, to be the very reverse of all of this. It is founded entirely on the two conceptions of the state of nature and the law of nature, and it is difficult to see how Locke could arrive at either of these conceptions from experience, unless his notion of the character of the process by which abstract ideas are to be formed was altogether different from what a student of his Essay on the Understanding would naturally have supposed it to be."[2]

In *The Metaphysics of Morals* Kant maintains that the rational concept of a right is directly related to the Idea of free will and so if a relevant criticism of his approach is to be offered it is important to be clear about the way in which he attempts to establish this connection. The key part of his claim reads: "…we know our own freedom (from which all moral laws, and so all rights as well as duties proceed) only through the *moral imperative*, which is a proposition commanding duty, from which the capacity for putting others under obligation, that is, the concept of right, can afterwards be explicated." The first part of this statement is a condensed form of the central argument of the *Groundwork* which holds that an indissoluble connection obtains between the Idea of a free will and a moral law in the form of the categorical imperative. In sum he argues as follows: that moral agency is inconceivable without the Idea of free will, the Idea under which all moral agents are compelled to act; that this Idea is "a pure concept of reason" [VI: 221] and that "all moral concepts have their have their seat and origin completely *a priori* in reason, and indeed in the most ordinary human reason just as much as in the most highly speculative. They cannot be abstracted from any empirical, and hence merely contingent cognitions" [IV: 411]; he claims that analysis of this Idea yields "a positive concept of freedom" [IV: 447] which reveals its relationship with a moral law such that "Upon this concept of freedom, which is positive (from a practical point of view) are founded unconditional practical laws, which are called moral" [VI: 221]; thus "a free will and a will under moral laws are one and the same" [IV: 447]; and that so far as the human moral agent is concerned this moral law presents itself as a categorical imperative whose original formulation (FUL) is: "Act according to a maxim that can at the same time be valid as a universal law." [VI: 226].

The second part of Kant's claim - from the categorical imperative to the concept of a right such as *ius inculpatae tutelae* - would presumably be established by him in the following way: FUL demonstrates that a maxim of murder - the intentional killing of an innocent person - *cannot* be willed as a universal permissive law and consequently one has a *moral* duty not to murder. This moral duty corresponds to a juridical *right* not to be murdered and since this right is regarded as innate it must also hold in the hypothetical pre-civil condition, the so-called 'state of nature'. Since the concept of a right is inseparable from an authorization to coerce [VI: 231] the only means of enforcing it outside of civil society would rest with the individual himself; it follows then that a *person* in a pre-civil condition as well as a *citizen* in a civil society has a right to blameless self-defence. Civil society does not create this right but only endorses and regulates it through coercive laws; it defends as lawful a plea of blameless self-defence against, say, a charge of homicide, and regulates this right by insisting that any use of force be proportionate to the level of threat. This deduction of *ius inculpatae tutelae* from FUL conforms exactly to Kant's claim that a right can be "explicated" from FUL and it is difficult to see any other way in which he could have gone about it.

Kant's contention that innate rights hold even in a pre-civil condition[3] is not only implicit in the concept of inalienability but made quite explicit in his 1786 review of Hufeland's *Essay on the*

Principle of Natural Night. Whilst praising this author in some respects Kant takes the opportunity to make it clear that Hufeland's point of departure is not the same as his. Kant begins by emphasising once again the relationship he claims between the Idea of free will and a moral law from which all duties and rights are said to derive: "The author, namely, does not hold principles of a free will, regardless of its object, to be sufficient to prescribe practical laws, and therefore to derive their obligatoriness. Hence for those formal rules he seeks a material, i.e. an object, which as the highest end of a rational being, which the nature of things prescribes to him, can be assumed as a postulate, and he posits it in the perfecting of *this end*. Hence the supreme practical principle is: further the perfection of all sensing beings, chiefly of rational beings, - hence also your own perfection; from which, then, we get the proposition: Prevent the diminution of perfection in others – but chiefly in you yourself (insofar as others might be the cause of it), which latter proposition obviously includes in itself a resistance, hence a coercion." Although Kant agrees with Hufeland that an authorization to coerce must hold in a state of nature he goes on to point out two serious difficulties in Hufeland's view. Firstly, since this supposed obligation to perfect oneself can rest only with each individual an authorization to coerce would remain the *exclusive* prerogative of each individual and no *part* of this authorization could be ceded to civil society – a society which, on Kant's view, can function only on the basis of self-imposed but nevertheless externally applied universal coercive laws. And secondly, since Hufeland's idea of perfectibility would seem to be without a determinate limit so too would the extent of the individual's authorization to use force in defence of his rights – a consequence, Kant maintains, that would present both the individual and society with insuperable problems.

Thus whilst agreeing with Hufeland that strictly moral questions have no place *in* a doctrine of right he remarks: "For the question is only under what conditions I can exercise the coercion without coming into conflict with the universal principles of right; whether the other may comport himself passively, or react according to the very same principles, is his business to investigate - as long, namely as everything is being considered in the state of nature; for in the civil state there is, corresponding to the judicial verdict which recognizes the right of one party, always an obligation of the opposing party." But from Hufeland's postulate of an obligation to perfectibility as the basis of a right to coerce it would seems to follow, Kant says, "...that one can *cede nothing* of one's right as permitting coercion, because this permission rests on an inner obligation to obtain the contested perfection for ourselves, if necessary with force. It also appears that on the assumed standard for authorization, the estimation of that to which I have a right, even in the commonest cases of life, must turn out to be so artificial that even the most practised understanding must find itself in continual bewilderment, if not in a downright impossible position, when it tries to make out how far its right might reach." [VIIIH: 128/9].

From the foregoing considerations one can conclude that the right of blameless self-defence is an integral part of authentic Kantian political philosophy and must be taken into account when considering his opposition to *eine Revolution*. For example, from this standpoint it would not be inconsistent to hold that the force employed by citizens in their self-defence against the violent acts of the Russian state was lawful whereas the opportunistic slogan of the Bolsheviks, "All Power to the Soviets!" was not.

Given the central position of FUL in Kant's political philosophy and the fashionable neo-kantian pretence that its role is only marginal it will be as well at this point to describe in more detail his own method of applying this fundamental ethical principle and to distinguish it clearly from the 'universalisation test' with which it is so often confused.

1. Kant's Application of FUL

Kant's original formulation of the categorical imperative is stated in the *Groundwork of the Metaphysics of Morals*: "I ought never to act except in such a way that I could also will that my maxim should become a universal law." [IV: 402]. The basic "principle of right" to which he refers in *Perpetual Peace* ten years later is stated in a similar way: "Act in such a way that you can will your maxim to become a universal law (irrespective of what the end in view may be)" [VIIIP: 377]. The relationship between these two formulations should be clear enough but there is an important difference in that the second includes the qualification "irrespective of what the end in view may be". On the basis of Kant's concept of "an end that is also a duty" [VI: 382] and of his description in the third *Critique* of his approach as "moral teleology" it has been argued elsewhere[4] that his ethical philosophy cannot be characterised as deontological but is in fact a unique form of teleological ethics distinct from all varieties of Consequentialism. It was also argued that on Kant's view FUL and other formulations of the categorical imperative already express an end – *humanity as an end in itself* - but an end grounded in the Idea of free will and qualitatively distinct from any contained in a hypothetical imperative. Whilst both formulations of FUL require that a maxim be tested to determine its suitability as a permissive universal law only the first commands that acting in accordance with duties arising from it ought to be done simply because one has a *moral* duty to do so. But for Kant a *duty of right* does not require this moral motivation, that is, respect for the moral law which makes an act a duty, but only that one acts in accordance with a practical law whatever one's reasons for doing so might be. As he puts it: "All duties are either duties of right (*officia iuris*), that is, duties for which external lawgiving is possible, or duties of virtue (*officia virtutis s.ethica*) for which external lawgiving is not possible. – Duties of virtue cannot be subject to external lawgiving simply because they have to do with an end which (or the having of which) is also a duty. No external lawgiving can bring about someone's setting an end for himself (because this is an internal act of the mind), although it may prescribe external actions that lead to an end without the subject making it his end." [VI: 239] Thus one person may refrain from murder because FUL demonstrates this to be immoral (and hence also unjust) whilst another may refrain only through fear of punishment – that is, not from respect for the end expressed in the principle itself but for the sake of some other, *extraneous*, end.

The claim that Kant does not seek to derive a wide range of moral and juridical duties from FUL is directly contradicted in all of his ethical works from the *Groundwork of the Metaphysics of Morals* onwards. Some remarks on the origin of the conventional belief can be found in the Conclusion to this essay but here it is sufficient to note the emphatic and far-reaching claims Kant himself makes on behalf of this principle: in the *Groundwork* [IV: 404] he describes this "first principle" as "a compass...well able to distinguish, in all cases that present themselves, what is good or evil, right or wrong – provided that, without the least attempt to teach it anything new, we merely make reason attend, as Socrates did, to its own principle; and how in consequence there is no need of science or philosophy for knowing what a man has to do in order to be honest and good, and indeed to be wise and virtuous."; in the *Critique* of *Practical Reason* [V: 9] the categorical imperative is described as a "formula" which defines accurately what is to be done "..for all duty in general"; and whilst referring in *The Metaphysics of Morals* [VI: 225] to "...the ability of our reason to determine choice by the mere idea that a maxim qualifies for the universality of a practical law" he writes: "The simplicity of this law in comparison with the great and various consequences that can be drawn from it must seem astonishing at first..." So leaving aside for the moment Kant's view of the general ethical significance of the categorical imperative[5] two key issues arise: firstly, since both the 1785 and 1795 versions of FUL require the testing of a maxim one has to consider exactly what Kant himself mean by a 'maxim', and secondly, how the procedure he describes is supposed to generate moral and juridical duties both to do and to forbear.

Perhaps the most instructive approach to both of these issues is to examine two typical 'puzzle maxims', the source of so much agonising in the neo-kantian literature. A puzzle maxim is said to be one that passes Kant's 'universalisation test' when it should not or fails to do so when it should. Some of these maxims involve obvious ethical issues whilst others seem trivial but in all cases they raise what are claimed to be insuperable problems for the categorical imperative at least in the form of FUL. An example of the first is given by MacIntyre (1990:46), "Persecute all those who hold false religious beliefs", which is said by its author to pass "Kant's test" since it can be "consistently universalized", and one of the second is given by Scanlon (1983) "To play tennis on Sunday mornings at 10.00 a.m." which is also said to fail 'Kant's test'. It should be noted at the outset that terms such as 'universalization' and 'universalizability' will not be found in any work of Kant's but in fact were introduced in the 1950's as part of R.M. Hare's Prescriptivism. But far more important is the implicit assumption involved in the concept of false positives and false negatives, ideas which obviously presuppose some ethical criterion independent of FUL and in virtue of which a particular prescription expressed by a maxim is held to be moral or immoral. No doubt many would regard MacIntyre's maxim as immoral and Scanlon's as not but today as in the past there are certainly those whose religious convictions lead them to take the opposite view. Yet in the voluminous literature on puzzle maxims one finds no mention at all of the implied ethical criterion by which this or that maxim is so emphatically claimed to be moral or immoral, and indeed without ever specifying whatever notion of this kind he happens to have in his mind Wood (2008:72) goes so far as to proclaim to the world that he has discovered an infallible method for producing a false positive: "An infallible recipe for producing a false positive is to formulate a maxim involving a kind of action that we know is contrary to duty but is presented in the maxim in such specific terms that even if the maxim were a universal law (or a law of nature), that law would foreseeably have no instances except the present (intuitively immoral) action. In that case, it could be no more difficult for the agent to will the maxim as a universal law than to will this action itself, and so any argument from the universalizability test would be either circular or its result inconclusive." Wood says that the first ingredient of his infallible recipe is a maxim involving "a kind of action that we know is contrary to duty" but he never gets round to explaining just how we are supposed to *know* that an action is contrary to duty. By what ethical criterion do we identify an action of this kind and identify it with that certainty required of an infallible recipe? For if this recipe is to do what it is said to do it must rely on some incontestable ethical criterion whose application is itself so certain in outcome that from it no false positive or negative could possibly be generated. And without that no infallible judgement can be made where FUL or any other putative ethical principle is concerned. Thus as it stands Wood's recipe is of no use to anyone else since he has yet to reveal to the world the precise nature of its first indispensable ingredient.

Before considering how Kant applies his own (explicit) ethical criterion it is important to understand his view not only of the form of a maxim but of how it originates and here Scanlon's example is particularly revealing. To Kant a maxim is neither an imperative nor a practical law but rather a subjective rule of conduct that an agent frames for himself and upon which he chooses or might choose to act: "A *maxim* is a subjective principle of volition; the objective principle (i.e., that which would also serve subjectively as the practical principle for all rational beings if reason had complete control over the faculty of desire) is the practical *law*." [IV: 402]. Kant makes it clear that in his view all maxims spring from desires and inclinations and thus signify *wants* of one kind or another [IV: 427], namely, "how the subject wants to act" [VI: 225], but whilst some maxims express desires that could in principle *also* be shared by all moral agents other maxims cannot and the function of FUL is to distinguish between the two. This basic relationship between maxims and desires is also clearly stated in the *Groundwork of the Metaphysics of Morals*. In practical philosophy, Kant writes, "...we have no need to set up an enquiry as to the reasons why anything pleases or displeases; how the pleasure of mere sensation differs from taste, and whether the latter differs from a universal approval by reason; whereon feelings of pleasure and displeasure are based; how from these feelings there arise desires and inclinations; and how from these in turn, with the co-operation of reason, there arise maxims." [IV: 427]. Even at this point a fundamental flaw in

Scanlon's example should be apparent although this passes undetected by those neo-kantian commentators like Herman (1993) and Schossberger (2008) who discuss it. As described by Herman, Scanlon's example runs as follows:

"B knows that the best time to play tennis is Sunday morning when her neighbours are in church. At all other times the courts are crowded. B acts on a maxim of playing tennis on Sundays at 10:00. If everyone acted as B does, the courts would be crowded on Sunday mornings as well as all other times. What makes B's maxim rational is her knowledge that others can be counted on not to act on the same maxim."[6] Herman remarks: "...we may not organize our tennis playing to take advantage of our neighbour's religious commitments. This unfortunate result follows from the "success condition" used in the practical interpretation. A maxim is impermissible if its *success* would be undermined by universal action on that maxim." Commenting on the same maxim Schossberger (2008: 373-4) writes: "But ordinary moral intuition tells us that there is nothing wrong with playing tennis on Sunday mornings: no one is harmed by this, even if the maxim is universalized. A false negative is generated – that is, we are told that something is wrong (playing tennis on Sundays) when actually it is permissible."

As usual the basis of this 'ordinary moral intuition' is left undisclosed but even so the unfortunate result arises only if one takes Scanlon's rather Kant's concept of a self-defeating maxim. The question for Kant is not 'What if everyone tries to act on this maxim at the same time?', but 'Is the desire expressed in the maxim one that in principle everyone could share?' And if it is then it becomes *permissible* – not obligatory - for anyone to act upon this maxim should they choose to do so. Now there is no practical impossibility in holding that everyone can *desire* to play tennis on Sunday mornings at 10.00 a.m. but there obviously is in maintaining that everyone could *act* on this maxim at the same time. Permission for anyone who wants to act in a certain way does not imply that everyone will act in that way any more than permission for anyone to park their car at a particular place and time implies that everyone will park their car in that place and at that time. Thus from Kant's point of view Scanlon confuses a desire to act in a certain way with the act itself, and it takes no great philosopher to realise that it is physically impossible for everyone who wants to play tennis on Sunday mornings at 10.00 a.m. to actually do so. And that is why in cases where demand might exceed supply the human mind has managed to devise ingenious systems of procedure described in such phrases as 'forming a queue', 'purchasing a ticket' or 'booking a tennis court in advance'. As described below, in Kant's terminology Scanlon's maxim counts as "morally indifferent" but the real importance of this characterisation only emerges when one considers MacIntyre's example of a 'false positive'.

The confusions generated by the 'universalisation test' are intensified in versions such as MacIntyre's in which a maxim is construed as an imperative and so either states or implies that if it *can* be willed as a universal law one has a *duty* to act upon it - in fact the exact reverse of Kant's own method where a duty arises only if a maxim *cannot* be willed as a permissive universal law. The difference between permissible and forbidden maxims is first drawn in the *Groundwork* [IV: 439] and elaborated in *The Metaphysics of Morals* [VI: 221]: "By categorical imperatives certain actions are *permitted* or *forbidden*, that is, morally possible or impossible, while some of them or their opposites are morally necessary, that is, obligatory. For those actions, then, there arises the concept of a duty..." From these remarks alone it is evident that Kant's method with FUL cannot be reduced to a simple permissibility test for maxims as Wood (1999:164), for example, insists. He writes: "FUL and FLN [the law of nature formulation – LAC] provide only tests for the *permissibility* of any given maxim, but do not tell us positively what kind of maxim we must act on." Whilst it is correct to say that FUL is indeed a test of permissibility Wood fails to recognise that it is the *lack* of permissibility from which all positive duties arise. His claim that the categorical imperative does not "tell us what kind of maxim we must act upon" is manifestly false since even in the *Groundwork* it is stated that from this imperative a moral agent has positive duties to act on maxims of not committing suicide and of not making false promises, and positive duties to act on maxims of developing one's talents and of being beneficent; duties which on Kant's application of FUL arise only because the contraries of these maxims *cannot* be willed as universal permissive laws.

The nature of a morally indifferent action is described in *The Metaphysics of Morals*[VI: 223]: "An action that is neither commanded nor prohibited is merely *permitted*, since there is no law limiting one's freedom (one's authorization) with regard to it and so too no duty. Such an action is called morally indifferent (*indifferens, adiaphoron, res merae facultatis*). The question can be raised whether there are such actions and, if there are, whether there must be permissive laws (*lex permissiva*), in addition to laws that command and prohibit (*lex praeceptiva, lex mandati, lex vetiti*), in order to account for someone's being free to do or not to do something as he pleases. If so, the authorization would not always have to do with an indifferent action (*adiaphoron*); for considering the action in terms of moral laws, no special law would be required for it." Kant maintains that permissive universal laws do occur as can be seen from the several examples he gives in *The Metaphysics of Morals*.

The relationship between these various concepts is set out in Kant's *Table of Categories of Freedom* in the *Analytic* of the second *Critique* [V: 66] and his application of FUL can be summarized in the following way starting from the two classes into which all of his illustrations fall; '*I want to do X*' (where X is say 'To make a false promise)), and '*I do not want to do Y*' (where Y is say 'To be beneficent'):-

In the first case: 'I want to do X'; Am I permitted to do X?; Can I will this maxim as a universal permissive law?'; If I can, my maxim is "morally indifferent" [VI: 223] and I am *permitted* to do X; if I cannot, I am *forbidden* to do X and now have a *duty* not to do X. Thus if my maxim is to make an insincere promise I have a duty not to act upon it. The same method applies to the second case where my maxim is 'I do not want to do Y'. If I can will this maxim as a universal permissive law I am permitted not to do Y, but if I cannot I am forbidden to act upon it and now have a *duty* to act on the contrary of my maxim, that is, I have a duty to do Y. Thus if my maxim is not to be beneficent I now have a duty to be beneficent. According to Kant it is in this way, and only in this way, that a duty to do or to forbear can arise; that is, only when a maxim *cannot* be willed as a universal permissive law.

The relationship between FUL and some of Kant's other formulations of the categorical imperative is not difficult to see: a maxim which can *also* serve as a practical rule for all moral agents is *objective* in virtue of its universality; since a maxim of this kind necessarily includes, and so in principle could have been willed by, any moral agent, it treats all moral agents in conformity with their rational nature (their humanity arising from the Idea of free will) as *ends in themselves*; in acting in accordance with FUL all moral agents become self-legislators subject only to laws made by themselves but which are universal; hence there arises, as Kant puts it, "..the idea of the will of every rational being as a will giving universal law"; and by such law-making a moral agent contributes so far as it lies within his power to the establishment of a possible *kingdom of ends*. Conversely, a maxim that cannot serve as a universal permissive law treats all persons (including oneself) merely as a means to one's own *purely* subjective ends, that is, solely as an instrument for the satisfaction of one's own *uniquely* personal desires.

In testing whether a maxim can serve as a universal law neo-kantians are accustomed to speak of 'contradictions in conception' and 'contradictions in volition', terms which suggest two separate and distinct criteria of permissibility such that a maxim might fail by one but succeed by the other. Again these are not Kant's terms. For him there is a single "canon of moral appraisal" [IV: 423], one that is indeed volitional but only in the sense of his broader holistic concept of a rational will (*Der Wille*): "We must *be able to will* that a maxim of our action become a universal law." [IV: 424]. Since a maxim that cannot be coherently thought as a universal permissive law cannot be rationally willed as such in the final analysis this canon must come down to the practical meaning of Kant's conception of a "contradiction in the will". It is here that one encounters his distinction between "self-love" and "rational self-love" [V: 73], one of the central but least considered themes in his moral philosophy. Self-love, a concept widely discussed in the 18th and early 19th centuries, is regarded by Kant as "natural and active in us even prior to the moral law" and said to promote the well-being and happiness of the individual. For Kant, self-love is an essential attribute of all finite rational beings, beings compelled to act under the Idea of free will but who also have desires and inclinations that can, and often do, conflict with duties arising from forbidden maxims. A moral agent who restricts his maxims to those that are morally permissible conducts his life in accordance with *"rational self-love"*, and perhaps the most striking example of a contradiction in the will occurs in Kant's fourth illustration in the *Groundwork* concerning the maxim of non-beneficence [IV: 423]: "For a will that decided this would conflict with itself, since many cases could occur in which one would need the love and sympathy of others and in which, by such a law of nature arisen from his own will, he would rob himself of all hope of the assistance he wishes for himself." A contradiction in the will thus arises from maxims that are literally *self-defeating* but not in the sense in which Scanlon and others use the same term. The extreme example of a maxim of this kind is one that counsels self-destruction, and Kant refers directly to the concept of self-love in his argument against suicide.

From these considerations it should be evident that the procedure described by MacIntyre as "Kant's test" is not the test that Kant himself describes and whilst the maxim "Persecute all those who hold false religious beliefs" may well pass MacIntyre's 'universalization' test it clearly fails on Kant's. For what counts as a false belief to one religious sect is a divinely revealed truth to another and neither MacIntyre's Augustinian Christians nor any member of a rival religious sect could will this maxim as a permissible universal law, a law that would only permit others to persecute him on the same grounds as he wishes to persecute them. Or to put it succinctly: 'I want to persecute others but I do not want others to persecute me'. It is because of such contradictions in the will that a moral agent has a duty not to act on maxims that prescribe, say, theft, rape or torture since *if* it were possible to will any one of these maxims as a universal permissive law it would entitle others to treat him in like fashion; the thief does not want to be stolen from (there really is no 'honour among thieves'), the rapist does not want to be raped, and the torturer does not want to be tortured. To use Kant's form of words in *Reflexion 8051* (see below) none of these acts can come forward in a just civil union and citizens are lawfully entitled to defend themselves, if necessary by the use of force, against any state power which attempts to impose them.[7]

2. Kant's Remarks on Revolution prior to 1793.

Kant's first major public statement on revolution, *On the Relationship of Theory to Practice in Political Right*, Section II of *On the Common Saying: 'This May be True in Theory, but it does not Apply in Practice'*, was published in the *Berliner Monatsschrift* in September 1793. In France it was the year which saw the execution of Louis XVI and the formation of the Committee of Public Safety, and the one which followed the withdrawal of the invading Prussian army after the engagement at Valmy and the formal proclamation of the French Republic. Prior to *Theory and Practice* Kant makes a number of brief references to revolution three of which figure prominently in the secondary literature where they have been taken to contradict the uncompromising position against a legal right to *eine Revolution* stated in *Theory and Practice*. In chronological order they are: (1) *Idea for a Universal History from a Cosmopolitan Point of View*, published in the *Berliner Monatsschrift* November 1784; (2) *An Answer to the Question: What is Enlightenment?*, published in the *Berliner Monatsschrift* December 1784; and (3) the unpublished *Reflexion 8051*, dated by Adickes[8] to 1785-1788. This is also the period during which Kant formulates the basic principles of his mature ethical philosophy beginning with the *Groundwork of the Metaphysics of Morals* in 1785 and continuing with the *Critique of Practical Reason* in 1788.

The *Universal History* consists of nine Propositions the eighth of which includes the expression *Revolution der Umbildung*. Comparing Kant's reference here to his later remarks on revolution in *Theory and Practice*, Beck (1971) writes: "..in his Idea for a Universal History published nine years earlier, even before the French Revolution, Kant had spoken of the hope that "after many reformative revolutions, a universal cosmopolitan condition ... will come into being." In a note to this remark Beck adds: "The words translated "reformative revolutions" (*Revolutionen der Umbildung*) do not suggest (as the English words may) that these revolutions were to be bloodless." Thus Beck, who seems to think that any revolution worthy of the name involves the spilling of blood, suggests that by *eine Revolution der Umbildung* Kant actually means *eine Revolution*. But if one assumes that in his *Universal History* it is Kant's train of thought that is the coherent one then Beck cannot be correct because Kant's fifth Proposition has already ruled this interpretation out. This Proposition states: "The greatest problem for the human species, the solution of which nature compels him to seek, is that of attaining a civil society which can administer justice universally." Elaborating on this Kant writes: "This purpose can be fulfilled only in a society which has not only the greatest freedom, and therefore a continual antagonism among its members, but also the most precise specification and preservation of the limits of this freedom in order that it can coexist with the freedom of others. The highest task which nature has set for mankind must therefore be that of establishing a society in which *freedom under external laws* would be combined to the greatest possible extent with irresistible force, in other words of establishing a perfectly *just civil constitution.*" Clearly, then, if a constitution of this kind is necessarily combined with *irresistible* force then revolution in the sense of *eine Revolution* is out of the question and decisively so. As noted earlier, "irresistible force" is a central term in Kant's conception of a just civil society and here and elsewhere it does not refer to any use of force by a citizen but specifically to force directed towards the violent overthrow of a constitution. Beck makes no mention of Kant's fifth Proposition, presumably because if he had done so it would conclusively show that the *Universal History* lends no support to the view that before *Theory and Practice* was published Kant supported the idea of *eine Revolution.*

In *What is Enlightenment?* the following passage occurs: "A revolution may well put an end to autocratic despotism and to rapacious or power-seeking oppression, but it will never produce a true reform in ways of thinking. Instead, new prejudices, like the one's that they replaced, will serve as a leash to control the great unthinking mass." It should also be evident that here Kant is not endorsing *eine Revolution* but rather recognising its ultimate futility. There was no shortage of examples in his own time where in the name of social progress one form of despotism and power-seeking oppression was merely replaced by another and always to the ultimate disadvantage of the people as a whole.

Reflexion 8051 is one of several notes written by Kant in his copy of Achenwall's *Juris Naturae,* a work published in 1753. Speaking in *Theory and Practice* of a supposed legal *right* of rebellion Kant quotes Achenwall as follows: "If the danger which threatens the commonwealth as a result of long endurance of injustices from the head of state is greater than the danger to be feared from taking up arms against him, the people may then resist him. It may use this right to abrogate its contract of subjection and to dethrone him as a tyrant...The people, in dethroning its ruler, thus returns to the state of nature." Kant rejects Achenwall's attempt to justify *eine Revolution* and *Reflexion 8051* appears to be an earlier statement of the same view but with one critical addition – Kant distinguishes here between the lawful and unlawful use of force by a citizen. Yet this is not the interpretation of *Reflexion 8051* given by Beck (1971) and also by Rosen (1993). The short extract cited by Beck is rendered by him as follows: "Force, which does not presuppose a judgment having the validity of law [*rechtskraftig Urtheil*] is against the law; consequently [the people] cannot rebel except in the cases which cannot at all come forward in a civil union, e.g., the enforcement of a religion, compulsion to unnatural sins, assassination, etc., etc." A similar version is given by Rosen (199:162/3) "...in a much-quoted remark Kant seems to licence rebellion in special circumstances: "[The private employment of] [f]orce, which does not presuppose a judgment having the validity of law, is against the law; consequently [the people] cannot rebel except in cases which cannot at all come forward in a civil union, e.g. the enforcement of religion, compulsion to unnatural sins, assassination, etc.etc." " According to Rosen: "...Kant appears to argue that if governments cross certain elementary boundaries of justice – such as enforcing observance of a religion or compelling citizens to commit grave moral offences – then rebellion may be justified." Beck himself regards *Reflexion 8051* as further confirmation that at one point

Kant did endorse the idea of *eine Revolution* but Rosen disagrees and remarks that one should be wary of this passage partly because, he writes, "Kant never saw fit to commit the same ideas to print, and this suggests that they do not represent his considered opinion, particularly since his published views are vastly different."

The most interesting feature of these two translations is their rendering of the key word *"wiedersetzen"* as meaning "to rebel". But Kant does not employ this word to denote either rebellion or *eine Revolution* and at the time in question "wiedersetzen" meant to *resist* or to *oppose* as it does in the modern German *widersetzen*. There is no justification for translating Kant's *wiedersetzen* in the way that Beck and Rosen do, and in the context of *Reflexion 8051* no reason to suppose that it could refer to anything other than the right of a citizen to resist or to oppose *by force* any attempt by a state to contravene the basic rights of its citizens. On this interpretation of *widersetzen* Rosen's translation would read: "[The private employment of] [f]orce, which does not presuppose a judgment having the validity of law, is against the law; consequently [the people] cannot *resist* except in cases which cannot at all come forward in a civil union, e.g. the enforcement of religion, compulsion to unnatural sins, assassination, etc.etc. " " This way of understanding Kant's *wiedersetzen* is consistent with his argument in *Theory and Practice* that a citizen has inalienable rights, rights he is lawfully entitled to enforce against anyone, including the state, who acts against them. This interpretation is also consistent with Kant's contention in the second part of *The Metaphysics of Morals* [VI: 235] that one of these inalienable rights is the right of *ius inculpatae tutelae*.

Unlike Beck Rosen appears to see Kant's point but since he also assumes that a right to self-defence is the same as a right to *eine Revolution* or a right to rebellion the wider political significance of *Reflexion 8051* is lost.

3. Kant's Remarks on Revolution in the *Religion* and *Theory and Practice*.

In 1793 Kant published two works which deal with this subject, *Religion Within the Limits of Reason Alone* and *On the Relationship of Theory to Practice in Political Right*, Section II of *On the Common Saying: 'This May be True in Theory, but it does not Apply in Practice'*. Both of these works draw on concepts and principles first formulated in the *Groundwork of the Metaphysics of Morals* published eight years earlier. The Preface to first edition of the *Religion* begins with these words: "So far as morality is based upon the conception of man as a free agent who, just because he is free, binds himself through his reason to unconditioned laws, it stands in need neither of the idea of another Being over him, for him to apprehend his duty, nor of an incentive other than the law itself, for him to do his duty...Hence for its own sake morality does not need religion at all (whether objectively as regards willing, or subjectively as regards ability to act); by virtue of pure practical reason it is self-sufficient. For since its laws are binding, as the highest condition (itself unconditioned) of all ends, through the bare form of universal legality of the maxims, which must be chosen accordingly, morality requires absolutely no material determining ground of free choice, that is, no end, in order either to know what duty is or to impel the performance of duty." [VI: 3/4].

These words echo the argument of the *Groundwork* and as stressed above it is clear from the *Religion* as it is from *Perpetual Peace* that Kant regards the universal law formulation of the categorical imperative as fundamental to his practical philosophy. In the third essay of the *Religion* Kant refers to this moral law as "divine", but of course not in its traditional theistic meaning but in the sense of an ethical principle absolutely or unconditionally binding. Thus in *The Metaphysics of Morals* [VI: 443/4] he writes of the "duty of religion" as the duty of "recognizing all our duties *as* divine commands," but "...this is not consciousness of a duty *to God*. For this idea proceeds entirely from our own reason and we ourselves make it...Hence we do not have before us, in this idea, a given being to whom we would be under obligation; for in that case its reality would first have to be shown (disclosed) through experience. Rather, it is a duty of a human being to himself to apply this idea, which presents itself unavoidably to reason, to the moral law in him, where it is of the greatest moral fruitfulness." The same point is emphasised in *The Conflict of the Faculties*: "...if God should really speak to man, man could still never *know* that it was God speaking. It is quite impossible for man to apprehend the infinite by his senses, distinguish it from sensible beings, and *recognize* it as such. But in some cases man can be sure that the voice he hears is *not* God's; for if the voice commands him to do something contrary to the moral law, then no matter how majestic the apparition may be, and no matter how it may seem to surpass the whole of nature, he must consider it an illusion...We can use, as an example, the myth of the sacrifice that Abraham was going to make by butchering and burning his only son at God's command (the poor child, without knowing it, even brought the wood for the fire). Abraham should have replied to this supposedly divine voice: "That I ought not to kill my good son is quite certain. But that you, this apparition, are God – of that I am not certain, and never can be, not even if this voice rings down to me from (visible) heaven."

Kant's distinction between duties which derive from the moral law and mere social conventions is also made explicit: "As soon as anything is recognized as a duty, even if it should be a duty imposed through the arbitrary will of a human law-giver, obedience to it is also a divine command. Of course one cannot call statutory civil laws divine commands; yet, when they are just, *obedience* to them is still a divine command. The saying: "We ought to obey God rather than men," signifies merely that when men command anything which in itself is evil (directly opposed to the law of morality) we dare not, and ought not, obey them. But conversely, when a politico-civil law, itself not immoral, is opposed to what is held to be a divine statutory law, there are grounds for regarding the latter as spurious, since it contradicts a plain duty and since [the notion] that it is actually a divine command can never, by any empirical token, be accredited adequately enough to allow an otherwise established duty to be neglected on its account." It was remarks of this nature, directed against the arbitrary 'duties' of the religious authorities, which led to the censoring of parts of the *Religion*. Again the qualifications here are clear enough: when laws 'are just', 'when anything is recognized as a duty', and when it is not 'directly opposed to the law of morality'. As we have seen, in the same vein Kant writes in the *Rechtslehre* [VI: 371]: "*Obey the authority that has power over you* (in whatever does not conflict with inner morality).."

Of all Kant's works on political philosophy Section II of *Theory and Practice*, *Against Hobbes*, seems to be the least understood. Although several commentators have noted Kant's statements on the *moral* limits of a citizen's obedience to executive authority there seems to be no understanding at all of his view on the *legal* limits of that authority in relation to his argument in support of inalienable human rights. In conventional treatments of *Theory and Practice* the main emphasis has always been upon Kant's denial of a legal right to revolution with little or no mention of the key point at issue with Hobbes, much less any examination of the origin and nature of the inalienable rights he defends in this work. Yet even on the question of revolution (*eine Revolution*) conventional views are misleading. Consider, for example, the following two remarks from *Theory and Practice* – the first has already been quoted - which must be read together:

"..if a public law is beyond reproach (i.e. *irreprehensible*) with respect to right, it carries with it the authority to coerce those to whom it applies, and conversely, it forbids them to resist the will of the legislator by violent means. In other words, the power of the state to put the law into effect is also *irresistible*, and no rightfully established commonwealth can exist without a force of this kind to suppress all internal resistance. For such resistance would be dictated by a maxim which, if it became general, would destroy the whole civil constitution and put an end to the only state in which men can possess rights.

"It thus follows that all resistance against the supreme legislative power, all incitements of the subjects to violent expressions of discontent, all defiance which breaks out into rebellion, is the greatest and most punishable crime in the commonwealth, for it destroys its very foundation. And even if the power of the state or its agent, the head of state, has violated the original contract by authorizing the government to act tyrannically, and has thereby, in the eyes of the subject, forfeited the right to legislate, the subject is still not entitled to offer counter-resistance. The reason for this is that the people, under an existing civil constitution, has no longer any right to judge how the constitution should be administered. For if we suppose that it does have this right to judge and that it disagrees with the judgement of the actual head of state, who is to decide which side is right? Neither can act as a judge of its own cause. Thus there would have to be another head above the head of state to mediate between the latter and the people, which is self-contradictory." [VIIIC: §2]

As Schwarz (1977) points out it is evident here that when read in context Kant is not rejecting resistance *per se* but only resistance directed towards the forcible overthrow of a constitution; "..all incitement of the subjects to *violent* expressions of discontent, all defiance *which breaks out into rebellion*", and so on and so on. That is why in the same essay Kant describes the view that the head of state is entitled to treat citizens as he pleases as "quite terrifying" and there could hardly be a more telling statement of his view that denying a legal right to *eine Revolution* does not mean consigning the citizen to the mercy of the state. On the theme of the just use of state power one should also mention here a further attempt by Beck to place Kant on the side of *eine Revolution*. This concerns the relationship between Kant's views on *eine Revolution* and those of Rehberg, someone who Beck chooses to describe as "one of Kant's disciples". He writes:

"Given what we know of Kant's theory of natural law and of the justification of positive law by reference to it – a theory as susceptible to a Lockean as to a Hobbesian development – it is easy to suppose that Kant could have asserted the right of resistance to a tyrannical government which denied autonomy to the legislation of the citizens. In fact, one of his disciples, August Wilhelm Rehberg, in the following issue of the Berlinische Monatsschrift, replied to Kant and drew precisely this conclusion from Kantian premises: 'If a system of *a priori* positive specifications of natural law is applied to the world of men, nothing less than a complete dissolution of present civil constitutions would follow. For according to such a system, only that constitution is valid which accords with the determination of the ideal of reason. In this case, no one of the existing constitutions could stand.... If these constitutions contradict ... the first requirements of a rational constitution, the human race is not only permitted, it is required, to destroy these constitutions which are opposed to the original moral law. The form of the constitution of the state is a matter of indifference, so long as complete equality is established; but to establish this, everything else must be sacrificed.-Thus the theory of revolution is a necessary consequence of the physiocratic system.' Kant spurned Rehberg's essay (without specifically mentioning the putative deduction of the right of rebellion), and his tentative justification of the Glorious Revolution of 1688 remained hidden in his notes. In his published works, there is only one half-hearted commendation for revolution (cited above) and one passage (later than the contribution to Biester's journal) which excuses, if it does not justify, revolution".

Leaving aside Beck's remark about the connection between the views of Kant, Locke and Hobbes on natural law and his persistent conflation of 'resistance' and 'revolution' the facts about the philosophical relationship between Kant and Rehberg are not difficult to establish. Although Beck declines to mention the fact Rehberg was an influential member of the Hanoverian Whigs who as mentioned earlier were admirers of Burke and like him deeply hostile to the idea of *eine Revolution*. As with some other intellectuals of the day Rehberg accepted the idea of a moral law but understood this in a way very different from Kant. For Rehberg this law was merely a negative ethical criterion which established only that rational moral and juridical principles are universal but nevertheless a law that was intrinsically incapable of generating determinate moral and juridical duties and most certainly not any particular form of constitution. Since for Rehberg the moral law was powerless in this sense the only possible specific guides to what is morally right or wrong and just or unjust are to be found in historically evolved traditional forms of social and political organisation – that is, they have to be derived empirically. Furthermore, Rehberg contends, it is a most dangerous error to attribute to reason a power it does not have and when allowed the wide scope claimed by Kant it is bound to have disastrous social consequences of the kind then to be seen in France. If one attempts like Kant to derive from the 'moral law' an ideal constitutional form nothing in the real world could possibly stand comparison with it and hence, as Rehberg puts it, "the human race is not only permitted, it is required, to destroy these constitutions which are opposed to the original moral law." In Rehberg's world view Kant was not the only philosopher to exaggerate the power of reason and in this respect Rousseau does not come off well either.

In the first instance then Rehberg was not attempting to derive the idea of *eine Revolution* "from Kantian premises" but rather attempting the exact opposite, and indeed he was soon to become one of the most influential German opponents of The French Revolution. Secondly, although Beck is correct in saying that Kant did not reply to Rehberg he does not give Kant's reasons for declining to do so nor does he report Kant's view that far from basing his ethical perspective on "Kantian premises" Rehberg's political standpoint was "infinitely" far from his own, grounded as it was in the empiricist ethical tradition. Biester, the editor of the *Berlinische Monatsschrift*, had written to Kant on March 4th 1794 with a copy of Rehberg's essay and inviting Kant to reply and on the 10th of April Kant writes back to Biester: "Mr Rehberg's essay "On the Relation of Theory to Practice" arrived only yesterday. In reading it, I found that, as regards the infinite disparity between rationalist and empiricist interpretations of the concept of right, the answering of his objections would take too *long*; with regard to his principle of right grounded on power as the highest source of legislation, the answering would be too *dangerous*; and in view of his already having decided in favour of the powers that be (as on page 122), the answering would be in vain…" Thus Beck not only misrepresents Kant but also Rehberg and it is difficult to believe he did not know that Rehberg's essay was in fact a criticism of Kant's approach to practical reason and also an emphatic rejection of *eine Revolution*. And if Beck honestly believed that Rehberg's argument was founded on "Kantian premises" then this does not speak highly for his own comprehension of the fundamental principles of Kant's ethical philosophy. Without examining the issue Sullivan (1989:245) simply regurgitates Beck's indefensible claim: "During Kant's lifetime, one of his followers did in fact argue that Kant's own theory not only permitted but required people to rebel against a government…But Kant refused to even acknowledge the existence of the essay."

To summarize the argument so far: (1). Kant's published works and correspondence between 1784 and 1798 demonstrate a consistent opposition to *eine Revolution*. The contrary view is based primarily upon a failure to recognise his distinction between *eine Revolution* and *eine Revolution des Volks* together with highly selective citations of his works taken out of context. Nor does the evidence support some system of compromise between the contradictory principles of *eine Revolution* on the one hand and an evolutionary process of reform on the other, as has been claimed by Williams (2003:26): "...revolution was not Kant's favoured method for bringing about political improvement. He much preferred reform, which he believed could secure the improvements towards a rational form of government without causing excessive and unnecessary harm." (2). Kant's opposition to *eine Revolution* does not leave the citizen defenceless against the violent acts of a state. The contrary view is based upon a failure to comprehend the ethical importance of his argument in support of inalienable rights and most especially the right of *ius inculpatae tutelae*.

The next major issue concerns the question of whether Kant's opposition to *eine Revolution* is contradicted by his views on The French Revolution.

Notes to Part I

1. "When an innocent man's life or property was faced with violence, Roman law demonstrated a pervasive respect for his right to self defence. It permitted threatened individuals to kill thieves, soldiers, and other violent attackers and to drive off or, if necessary, to kill creditors or government agents who had come to seize property illegally. In many instances it recognized, expressly or by implication, an individual's ability to own or possess weapons as a means of procuring his self defence." Tysse, W: <u>The Roman Legal Treatment of Self Defense and the Private Possession of Weapons in the *Codex Justinianus*.</u>" See also Book III, Title XXVII "When it is permitted to avenge oneself or (a breach of) public fidelity without a judge" and Bas. 60.39.16, 3.27.1: "It is better to forestall, rather than to punish the deed". Blume, F.H. *Annotated Justinian Code*. Ed. Kearley, T., University of Wyoming, 2010.

2. Fitzjames S: <u>Locke's Essay on the Human Understanding</u>. *Horae Sabbaticae*, volume 2, London, Macmillan, 1892. This acute observation is overlooked by later writers when comparing Kant and Locke on rights and revolution. A recent example of this kind is Flikschuh, K. <u>Reason, Right, and Revolution: Kant and Locke.</u> *Philosophy & Public Affairs*, 2008, vol. 36, no. 4, 375-404. Fitzjames Stephen's essay is reprinted in Yolton, J.S. *A Locke Miscellany*. Thoemmes, Bristol, 1990. The quoted remark is on pp.197/8 of this edition.

3. Flikschuh (*op.cit.*) writes: "In Kant's pre-civil condition individuals have valid *claims* to Right (*Recht*) but lack relevant enforcement powers. Legitimate enforcement of pre-civil rights claims is possible only in the civil condition." This is misleading since it seems to imply that *actual* rights cannot exist in a state of nature. At a later point it becomes clear that this is indeed what Flikschuh is claiming: "I also suggested that there are no natural rights in Kant's pre-civil condition", and again: "Given the absence of natural rights in Kant..". And finally she refers to "..Kant's abandonment of natural law thinking, including natural rights..". Although Flikschuh claims that her paper is based on a "Kantian perspective" the view of natural rights she presents is not Kant's. In his view an innate right "...is that which belongs to everyone by nature, independently of any act that would establish a right..." [VI: 237] and here he treats 'innate' and 'natural' as cognate terms and this also includes his use of 'inalienable'. If 'Right' in Flikschuh's "claims to Right" means a claim to Justice then it fails to take account of Kant's argument that all such claims are grounded in *actual* rights although rights that are only provisional in a state of nature since there is no mechanism by which they can be collectively enforced. In fact Kant maintains that if an actual right could not exist in a pre-civil condition it could not exist in a civil one either, and in the transition from a pre-civil to a civil condition all that happens is that a right which is only provisional in the former becomes established and guaranteed by law in the latter. Thus in speaking of *acquired* rights he says: "It is true that the state of nature need not, just because it is natural, be a state of *injustice* (*iniustus*), of dealing with one another only in terms of the degree of

force each has. But it would still be a state *devoid of justice (status iustitia vacuus)*, in which when rights are in *dispute (ius controversum)*, there would be no judge competent to render a verdict having rightful force……If no acquisition were cognized as rightful even in a provisional way prior to entering the civil condition, the civil condition itself would be impossible. For in terms of their form, laws concerning what is mine or yours in the state of nature contain the same thing that they prescribe in the civil condition, insofar as the civil condition is thought of by pure rational concepts alone. The difference is only that the civil condition provides the conditions under which these laws are put into effect (in keeping with distributive justice). – So if external objects were not even *provisionally* mine or yours in the state of nature, there would also be no duties of right with regard to them and therefore no command to leave the state of nature." [VI: 312]. If all this is true of acquired rights then by their very nature it must be no less so with rights that Kant regards as innate.

4. Callender, L.A. (2008): <u>Kant's Moral Teleology and 'Consequentialism'</u>. In *Recht und Frieden in der Philosophie Kants, Akten des X. Internationalen Kant-Kongresses.* Band 3, pp.33-41.

5. A recent paper by Geiger (2010) is an excellent example of the confusion between the 'universalisation test' and Kant's method with FUL and also of the failure to understand the proper meaning of Kant's "contradiction in the will". Like Wood Geiger claims that the categorical imperative only tells us what we already 'know', which of course leaves hanging in the air the question of exactly

how we are supposed to know what we are supposed already to know: <u>What is the Use of the Universal Law Formula of the Categorical Imperative?</u> *British Journal for the History of Philosophy* 18 (2), 2010. On the other hand, Millgram (2003) raises the important question of whether what now passes for 'Kant's test' is actually Kant's test and he writes: "We ought first to develop a deeper diagnosis of what has gone wrong with the Categorical Imperative, first formulation; but to come by that, we will need a better handle on the philosophical motivations of the New Kantian position than we now have, starting with an explanation of why an agent wills the universalization of his maxim (so that the contradictions exhibited by the CI-procedure are contradictions *in* the agent's will). I do not think this question can be successfully pursued without turning from the New Kantians back to Kant himself..": <u>Does the Categorical Imperative Give Rise to a Contradiction in the Will?</u> *The Philosophical Review.* Vol. 112, No. 4 (October 2003). A fuller discussion of the problems associated with the 'CI-procedure' will be found in Callender, L.A: <u>Puzzle Maxims and the Formula of Universal Law</u>, 11th International Kant Congress, Pisa, 2010.

6. Scanlon, T.M. <u>Kant's Groundwork: From Freedom to Moral Community</u>. Lecture No. 2, Harvard University, 1983.

7. Only some innate rights have been briefly mentioned here but an essay specifically dealing with Kant's approach to inalienable rights is in preparation.

8. *Reflexion 8051* [XIX] is given by Adickes as "Ψ^3. J189"; the Greek letter refers to 1785-1788 and the "J" to Achenwall's *Juris Naturae*.

PART II
FRANCE: NOTES ON CONSTITUTIONAL CHANGE IN 1789

1. Absolute and Constitutional Monarchy.

Philosophers influenced by Kant's claim that a republic is the ideal constitutional form and by his remarks on "the revolution of a gifted people" in France often seem to assume that the origin of the conflicts in that country in 1789 is to be found in an opposition between monarchism and republicanism. The declared position of the majority of Third Estate Deputies and of those who formed the National Assembly on 17th June in that year does not support this view. Republicanism had no significant following in 1789 and did not become a major political issue until after the flight of the royal family towards the Austrian frontier in the summer of 1791. Schama (1989:555) describes the political impact of this event: "Someone posted a placard against the gates of the Tuileries palace reading "Maison à louer" (House to let). The more telling reaction, however, was among relatively moderate politicians whose faith in a viable *active* constitutional monarchy was irreversibly undermined. Condorcet, for example, was immediately converted to republicanism, hitherto the preserve of only the wilder zealots of the Cordeliers, and discussed with Brissot and Tom Paine plans to set up a journal actively campaigning for an end to the monarchy." But in 1789 the issue was not the abolition of the monarchy as such but rather the establishment of a constitutional monarchy in place of the formal absolute monarchy then prevailing. This was the common standpoint of people like Lafayette who had fought on the side of the colonists in the American War of Independence and of individuals such as Robespierre who would later declare themselves implacable opponents of monarchy as an institution. Scurr (2006:106/7) describes the general attitude towards the monarchy in 1789: "Publicly, Robespierre was working hard to establish a constitutional monarchy. Like everyone else he could see that the presence of Louis XVIth made it impossible to draft a constitution with a wholly new executive power, as the Americans had done in their revolution. Instead the Assembly had to compromise and design a new role for their existing monarch. The radical deputies did so grudgingly and with a great many suspicions. Even so, there was never any suggestion in the Assembly (and almost none outside it either) that the king should simply be deposed, still less executed, and France declared a Republic." This is equally true of Sieyès, author of *What is the Third Estate?*, a document regarded by historians as the most influential political pamphlet of the period. Sieyès did not direct his attack against the king, much less against the monarchy as an institution, but against the power of the nobility in the Church, the Law and the Army:

"If you consult history in order to verify whether the facts agree or disagree with my description, you will discover, as I did, that it is a great mistake to believe that France is a monarchy. With the exception of a few years under Louis XI and under Richelieu and a few moments under Louis XIV when it was plain despotism, you will believe you are reading a history of a *Palace* aristocracy. It is not the King who reigns; it is the Court. The Court has made and the

Court unmade; the Court has appointed ministers, and the Court has dismissed them; the Court has created posts and the Court has filled them..And what is the Court but the head of this vast aristocracy which overruns every part of France, which seizes on everything through its members, which exercises everywhere every essential function in the whole administration? So that in its complaints the people has grown used to distinguishing between the monarch and those who exercise power. It has always considered the King as so certainly misled and defenceless in the midst of the active and all-powerful Court that it has never thought of blaming him for all the wrongs done in his name."[1]

Thus in the first instance one has to consider not the conversion of a monarchy to a republic but rather the conversion of an absolute into a constitutional monarchy and the particular way in which this occurred. The French Republic was not formally proclaimed until September 1792 following the withdrawal of the invading Prussian forces at Valmy and Kant's remarks in the *Rechtslehre* concern the assumption of sovereign and executive authority by the National Assembly in the period between May and June of 1789, the critical step in the formation of the constitutional monarchy.

The principles governing the exercise of sovereign and executive power by the monarchy of Louis XVIth had been stated in the most uncompromising terms by Louis XVth in 1766 when rejecting any interference in these matters by the judicial high courts:

"To attempt to establish such pernicious innovations as principles is to affront the magistrature, to betray its interests and to ignore the true, fundamental laws of the state, as if it were permissible to disregard the fact that in my person alone lies that sovereign power whose very nature is the spirit of counsel, justice and reason. From me alone the courts receive their existence and authority. The fullness of this authority, which they exercise in my name only, remains permanently vested in me, and its use can never be turned against me. Legislative power is mine alone, without subordination or division. It is by my sole authority that the officers of my courts effect, not the creation of the law, but its registration, promulgation and execution, and that they have the right of remonstrance, as is the duty of good and faithful counsellors. Public order in its entirety emanates from me. I am its supreme guardian. My people are one with me, and the rights and interests of the nation – which some dare to make into a body separate from the monarch – are of necessity united with my own and rest entirely in my hands."[2]

Such was the form of the absolute monarchy but as the defensive nature of this declaration indicates the substance was rather different. The *ancien régime* with its vested interests, hereditary privileges, inequitable taxes and arbitrary laws had come under increasing pressure long before the first meeting of the Estates General on 5th May 1789 but it was the financial crisis culminating on the 16th August 1788 with the suspension of payments on the vast loans contracted in pursuit of French imperial ambition which presented a real opportunity for constitutional change. Attempts by the central authority to bring about fiscal and administrative reform had encountered strong resistance from each Assembly of Notables in 1788 as well as from the *parlements* and the central administration with its complex web of interlocking interests was unwilling to force these measures through. At this crossroads a thoughtful courtier at Versailles might well have recalled the words of the Roman historian Livy when he speaks of: "..the dark dawning of our modern day when we can neither endure our vices nor face the remedies needed to cure them." As some of the king's ministers knew only too well the alternative policy carried even greater risks, for whilst confronting the economically and politically powerful three per cent of the population would be difficult enough opening the door to the Third Estate and the rest of the population it nominally represented could prove altogether unmanageable. Add to this the economic distress of large sections of the population described by contemporaries like Arthur Young and amply documented by historians since and it is clear that social tensions in France had reached crisis point. The calling of the Estates-General was in effect an unmistakeable public recognition of the inherent structural weaknesses of the *ancien régime* and the largely pretentious character of absolutist royal authority.

The military commander may inflate the strength of an opposing force so as to render his victory all the more glorious but without wishing to diminish the achievements of the National Assembly in the spring of 1789 it is important not to exaggerate the power and stability of the existing order. For it was not as though there was a deliberate attempt to overthrow the monarchy by force of arms but rather that the inherent fragility of the *ancien régime* rendered it increasingly susceptible to determined although largely passive resistance. The bare facts about the events which followed the first meeting of the Estates-General are well known and whilst opinions differ as to their relative significance they have not been challenged by any historian; after weeks of largely fruitless negotiations designed to unite the three orders in a common enterprise of constitutional reform Sièyes proposed that the Third, now calling itself the 'Commons', should proceed on its own. With the support of some members of the clergy and the nobility the Commons declared itself the National Assembly on June 17th and decreed the abolition of taxes and their immediate re-instatement as an interim measure. Furet (1988:63) describes these political and constitutional changes as follows: "By the use of this name alone, the Third estate relegated to the past the whole of the society of orders, and created a new power, independent of the king. The next day, it assigned itself the vote on taxation and placed the state's creditors 'under the guard of the honour and uprightness of the French nation'.. Truly a different sovereignty had just been baptized: the Revolution had been born." Doyle (2002:105) describes the same events in these words: "Target and Le Chapelier, the leading Breton deputy, proposed that all existing taxes be declared illegal but provisionally sanctioned until a new system could be devised. Authorization would lapse if ever the Assembly ceased to meet. The implications were clear, but carried unanimously. The Assembly was claiming sovereignty, and inviting taxpayers to defy any government which tried to dissolve it. The challenge now was not merely to the other two orders, but to royal authority itself. As the British ambassador (a duke) reported to his foreign secretary (another) the next day: "If

His Majesty once gives His decided approbation of the proceedings, such as they have hitherto been, of the Tiers-Etat, it will be little short of laying His crown at their feet." "

No doubt to the dukes this foreshadowed the end of the monarchy but to the Deputies themselves it did not for so far as they were concerned all of this had been accomplished without any direct threat to that institution. This is evident from their acceptance by a majority of 576 to 1 of the Decree that *included* the famous Tennis Court Oath but which *also* enjoined the National Assembly "to maintain the true principles of monarchy". This important fact goes unmentioned by adherents of the 'Jacobino-Marxist Vulgate' like Soboul and even by historians such as Furet, Doyle and Schama - a singular omission which creates the impression that the defiant stance adopted by the National Assembly was far more radical in intent than was the case. As reported in the *Gazette National, ou le Moniteur universel* published later that year the key part of the meeting on 17th June proceeded as follows under its President Jean-Sylvain Bailly:

"Bailly: I do not need to tell you in what a grievous situation the Assembly finds itself; I propose that we deliberate on what action to take under such tumultuous circumstances.

"M. Mounier offers an opinion, seconded by Messieurs Target, Chapelier, and Barnave; he points out how strange it is that the hall of the Estates General should be occupied by armed men; that no other locale has been offered to the National Assembly; that its president was not forewarned by other means than letters from the Marquis de Brézé, and the national representatives by public posters alone; that, finally, they were obliged to meet in the Tennis Court of Old Versailles street, so as not to interrupt their work; that wounded in their rights and their dignity, warned of the intensity of intrigue and determination with which the king is pushed to disastrous measures, the representatives of the nation bind themselves to the public good and the interests of the fatherland with a solemn oath.

"This proposal is approved by unanimous applause.

"The Assembly quickly decrees the following:

"The National Assembly, considering that it has been called to establish the constitution of the realm, to bring about the regeneration of public order, and to maintain the true principles of monarchy; nothing may prevent it from continuing its deliberations in any place it is forced to establish itself; and, finally, the National Assembly exists wherever its members are gathered.

"Decrees that all members of this assembly immediately take a solemn oath never to separate, and to reassemble wherever circumstances require, until the constitution of the realm is established and fixed upon solid foundations; and that said oath having been sworn, all members and each one individually confirm this unwavering resolution with his signature.

"Bailly: I demand that the secretaries and I swear the oath first; which they do immediately according to the following formula:

"We swear never to separate ourselves from the National Assembly, and to reassemble wherever circumstances require, until the constitution of the realm is drawn up and fixed upon solid foundations.

"All the members swear the same oath between the hands of the president."[3]

This Decree is undoubtedly a declaration of sovereignty for if it now devolved upon the National Assembly to draw up a constitution of the realm "fixed upon solid foundations", and moreover one in which the exact role of the monarchy would also be decided, then it is clear that the National Assembly now regarded itself as the sole repository of sovereign authority. It is also important to note the political significance of the phrase concerning the national representatives who, "wounded in their rights and their dignity, warned of the intensity of intrigue and determination with which the king is pushed to disastrous measures". This is a direct reference to the well-founded belief both in and outside of the National Assembly that the main opposition to reform of the monarchy as an institution came not from the king but from his brothers, the queen, and certain ministers other than Necker, Director-General of Finances. This opposition, which was soon to assume a military character, became a dominant theme in the events of the following three weeks but up to 20th June the overt political conflict was a battle of wills and certainly not a battle of arms. In his *Memoirs* (vol.1: 164/5) Bailly sums up his view of the constitutional change on the 20th June: "The government could not help but notice that this act was taking over the authority which, up to that day, was uniquely royal, and was putting it into the hands of the nation and of its legitimate representatives." This was also the view of other observers at the time, including Arthur Young who published his *Travels in France* in 1792. He too had no doubt about the constitutional import of the Tennis Court Oath and in Paris on 21st June 1789 he writes:

"The present moment is, of all others, perhaps that which is most pregnant with the future destiny of France. The step the commons have taken of declaring themselves the national assembly, independent of the other orders, and of the king himself, precluding dissolution, is in fact an assumption of all authority in the kingdom. They have at one stroke converted themselves into the long parliament of Charles I. It needs not the assistance of much penetration to see that if such a pretension and declaration are not done away, king, lords, and clergy are deprived of their shares in the legislature of France. So bold, and apparently desperate a step, full in the teeth of every other interest in the realm, equally destructive to the royal authority, by parliaments and the army, can never be allowed. If it is not opposed, all other powers will lie in ruins around that of the common. With what anxious expectation must one therefore wait to see if the crown will exert itself firmly on the occasion, with such an intention to an improved system of liberty, is absolutely necessary to the moment!

All things considered, that is, the characters of those who are in possession of power, no well digested system and steady execution are to be looked for."[4]

There is no suggestion in this or any other contemporary account that the constitutional change on 20th June was brought about by the use or threat of force on the part of the National Assembly. Young then went to a performance of Hamlet.

2. The Séance Royale, 23rd June

The battle of wills continued in the Royal Session of the 23rd June, called by the king in an attempt to reach some compromise but without acknowledging the National Assembly's claim to sovereignty. He put forward a list of reforms of which Doyle (2002:106) writes: "In fact the programme put forward by the king was quite imaginative, and most observers agreed, at the time and later, that if it had been put forward in May it would have been generally acclaimed. In a thirty-five point declaration he promised that in future no taxes and loans would be raised without the consent of the Estates-General, and that several unpopular taxes would be abolished or modified. He promised to abolish arbitrary imprisonment, forced labour on the roads, and serfdom. He announced the general establishment of provincial estates. But he also declared all feudal rights to be inviolable property, and he merely urged, and did not order, the nobility and clergy to give up their fiscal privileges." Some of the proposed reforms appear to go even further, such as introducing the idea of equality of taxation.

Article 12, for example, states: "...the king desires that the name *taille* be abolished in his realm, and that this tax be joined with the *vingtième* and all other land taxes, or that it be replaced in some manner, but always according to just and equal proportions, and without distinction of state, standing or birth...". The same might be said of the proposed reforms to the legal system as foreshadowed in Article 28: "...his majesty will examine all projects presented to him concerning the administration of justice, and means to perfect civil and criminal laws with scrupulous attention..."[5]

It is well-known that the list of proposed reforms was preceded and followed by a proclamation of the king which challenged the National Assembly's claim to sovereignty and also sought to reverse the changes in the organisation of the Estates that had taken place by 20th June: "Consider, Sirs, that none of your projects, none of your arrangements can have the force of law without my special approbation; I am the natural guarantor of your respective rights; all of the orders of the state may rely on my equitable impartiality. All defiance on your part will be gross injustice...I order you, Sirs, to separate immediately and to return tomorrow morning to the rooms assigned to your order to resume meetings."[6] The king then left followed by most of the clergy and the nobility and Dreux-Brézé, the Master of Ceremonies, attempted to get the Deputies to leave by declaring: "Gentlemen, you know the king's intent'. Furet (1992:64) interprets what happened next in this way: "The Revolution found three Roman phrases to express the new era. Bailly: 'The assembled nation cannot take orders.' Sieyès: 'You are today what you were yesterday.' Mirabeau: 'We shall not leave our places save at bayonet point.' Had Louis XVIth the means of imposing his policy in those decisive days? He did not even try. From then on, the resistance of the privileged was broken down by successive defections. On 27th June the king himself accepted the *fait accompli* by inviting 'his faithful clergy and his faithful nobles' to join with the Third Estate. In the evening, Paris was illuminated. The National Assembly had become a constituent body."

So what is to be made of this 'Revolution' and the stance adopted by Bailly, Sieyès and Mirabeau? Defiant yes, but in terms of *eine Revolution* hardly indicative of a revolutionary posture. In fact even Mirabeau's colourful pronouncement was too much for Bailly who immediately interjects to say that the king's proclamation required a more "measured" response. After all, he says, Dreux-Brézé was only doing his duty in relaying the voice of the king; had he uttered any menacing words? And who had spoken of bayonets or of force? (*Memoirs*, vol. 1:215). To Furet 'Revolution' has only one meaning but even when one accepts that a revolution of some description had occurred between the 10th and the 20th of June it would be fanciful in the extreme to compare the France of June 1789 with, say, the Russia of October 1917. Although important in its own way one cannot sensibly describe the events in Versailles during that time as ten days that shook the world.

Nevertheless, Bailly continued, the king had no right to demand a reversal of the constitutional change and in a re-affirmation of the Tennis Court Oath proposed by Mirabeau the National Assembly again declared the inviolability of its Deputies. Speaking on this specific point Bailly remarks: "If the Assembly was acting firmly and courageously in taking useful precautions against the ministry, if it was arming itself against its despotism, it was, however, of one heart and spirit with the King, and had no intention to do anything against his legitimate authority; the Assembly had even taken the precaution of declaring in its decree that one of its duties was to maintain the true principles of the monarchy, in order to prove to everybody that whatever could be considered hostile in its advances, was directed against despotism, and not against the monarchy." Speaking of the 23rd and the 27th of June Young was also of the opinion that the 'revolution' was at an end: "The whole business now seems over and the revolution complete. The king has been frightened by the mobs into overturning his own act of the Séance Royale, by writing to the presidents of the orders of the nobility and clergy, requiring them to join the commons - full in the teeth of what he had ordained before. It was represented to him, that the want of bread was so great in every part of the kingdom, that there was no extremity to which the people might not be driven: that they were nearly starving, and consequently ready to listen to any suggestions, and on the *qui vive* for all sorts of mischief: that Paris and Versailles would inevitably be burnt; and in a word, that all sorts of misery and confusion would follow his adherence to the system announced in the Séance Royale."[7] This dramatic capitulation did not result from the use or threat of force by the National Assembly and there is no evidence that this body or the one which succeeded it in July ever embarked on such a policy.

There are differing accounts of the king's response to Dreux-Brézé's report[8] but what cannot be doubted is the effect of the intransigence displayed by the National Assembly. Developments between June 23rd and July 14th, some military others constitutional, confirm that although about to be severely tested sovereign and legislative authority was now in the hands of the National Assembly. To take the constitutional points first. On 9th July the deputies voted to call themselves the National Constituent Assembly and established a committee to draw up the principles of a constitutional monarchy. In the debates which began in earnest in August and September of 1789 one cannot help noticing a certain surreal quality to some of the contributions for taken at face value it seems that some Deputies had not yet come to terms with the new constitutional realities. This is especially evident in the discussions about whether the king should have some kind of legislative veto. According to Mirabeau and the '*monarchiens*' the king should have an absolute veto, to others that he should have only a suspensory or delaying veto, and to those like Robespierre that the king should have no veto at all. But since all were agreed that this issue was to be decided by a vote in the Constituent Assembly and nowhere else then even by implication it was this body and this body alone which now regarded itself as the sole repository of sovereign and legislative power. In the event the *monarchien* position was rejected by the Constituent Assembly in September of 1789 and the king granted a suspensory veto by a majority of around two to one. The other important constitutional development in that year concerned the *Declaration of the Rights of Man and of the Citizen* and although not formally adopted until 26th

August its basic principles were agreed on the 11th July. Lafayette, now vice-president of the Constituent Assembly, presented the draft on which he had been working with Jefferson and this hurried change in the timetable of proceedings is explained by Paine (1985:54): "The particular reason for bringing it forward at this moment (M. de Lafayette has since informed me) was, that if the National Assembly should fall in the threatened destruction that then surrounded it, some traces of its principles might have the chance of surviving the wreck."

The military development, which began even before the Séance Royale, has also been well documented. Some frontier regiments had been ordered up on the 22nd June and after the unexpected outcome of the 23rd their numbers were increased on the 26th and over the next two weeks. Bailly was not so naive as to suppose that the new constitutional powers would go unchallenged and like many others saw the military threat as a direct response to the events beginning on June 10th when Sieyès had first proposed that the Third Estate should proceed on its own. Recalling on 8th July the king's proclamation of the 23rd June he records the general view of the Deputies at the time: "…perhaps the National Assembly will be dissolved ... since the King did declare that '*I alone will do the good for my peoples; alone I will consider myself to be their true representative.*' Bailly then adds: "This arbitrary coup of absolute authority, so strange under such circumstances, would have been backed up by those 20 or 30,000 men assembled with their artillery." (*Memoirs*, vol.1:299). Paine (1985:52), who was in contact at the time with leading members of the Assembly, tells of the week before July 14th: "...it was discovered that a plot was forming, at the head of which was the Count d'Artois, the King's youngest brother, for demolishing the National Assembly, seizing its members, and thereby crushing by a *coup de main*, all hopes and prospects of forming a free government." And speaking of the king's protestations that the only purpose of these troops was the maintenance of public order Schama (1989:377) writes: "All this was the classic preparatory language of the military *coup d'état*. The King even added a gratuitous suggestion of removing the Assembly to Noyons or Soissons should "conditions" make its work untenable at Versailles!". The evidence points unmistakeably to a coup planned for around 16th July if the Assembly did not back down from its stand at the Séance Royale. But what is a *coup d'état* if it is not a violent attempt to seize power from those who already hold it?

The expectations aroused by the announcement in August 1788 that the Estates-General would be convened the following Spring undoubtedly exacerbated age-old social antagonisms and traditional forms of protest like bread riots in the cities and confrontations, sometimes violent, between peasants and wealthy land-owners in the countryside. Disturbances of this kind were not peculiar to 1789 but there is no doubt that the intervening months saw increasing outbreaks of lawlessness throughout the country as royal authority and control, further undermined by the particularly severe winter of 1788, began to evaporate. Yet so far as is known none of this assumed a 'revolutionary' character in the sense of *eine Revolution*. Even the well-publicised attacks in April of 1789 on the property of the Parisian wallpaper manufacturer Réveillon and the salt merchant Henriot were prompted by rumours of cuts in wages, and although in the gathering mood of defiance these protests went much further than usual they cannot be interpreted as part of a developing 'revolutionary' enterprise if by this is meant an attempt at *eine Revolution*. Doyle (2002: 98/99) remarks: "The rioters were known to have cheered the names of the king, Necker, and the third estate. But they had also shouted 'down with the rich!' as they sacked prominent citizen's property, and the full force of authority had been deployed too late to prevent them. The capital must have appeared to the deputies even more disturbed than their native provinces." No doubt popular pressure imbued the National Assembly with a greater sense of urgency, but so far as it goes the evidence does not support the view that any of this was directed towards the violent overthrow of the monarchy as an institution. However these disturbances, said by some at the time to be the work of *agents provocateurs* in the pay of the Ministry, or of the king's cousin the duc d'Orléans or even agents of the British government did see the appearance of ideas decidedly alien to what Kant himself refers to as a revolution of the people. The connection between the first meeting of the Estates-General and a growing willingness to defy municipal and central authority was well illustrated in the Réveillon incident by a crowd which, as Schama (1989:328) writes, carried "a mock gallows to which was attached the hanging effigy of Réveillon and a placard proclaiming 'Edict of the Third Estate Which Judges and Condemns the Above Réveillon and Henriot to be Hanged and Burned in a Public

Square' ". It was attitudes of just this kind which would be unleashed on 14th July by the threatening coup.

In early July the Constituent Assembly attempted to deal with the problem of food shortages and public order and to consider its response to the military threat. On the latter issue questions were raised: What was the real purpose of the troops now encircling Paris and dug in at strategic points within it ? Why twenty thousand or more? Why foreign regiments like the Swiss Salis-Samade and the German Royal-Allemand and even irregulars like the central and east European Pandours, specialists in unconventional warfare and notorious for their brutality? Less than a quarter of the French army was composed of foreign troops and yet almost half of those around Paris and Versailles were said to be from these regiments. And why all the artillery? In his typically vivid fashion Carlyle (1837:184/5) describes the menacing situation in Paris at the time: "...what means this 'apparatus of troops'? The National Assembly can get no furtherance for its Committee of Subsistences; can hear only that, at Paris the baker's shops are besieged; that, in the Provinces, people are 'living on meal-husks and boiled grass.' But on all highways there hover dust-clouds, with march of regiments, with the trailing of canon: foreign Pandours, of fierce aspect; Salis-Samade, Esterhazy, Royal-Allemand; so many of them foreign; to the number of thirty thousand – which fear can magnify to fifty; all wending towards Paris and Versailles! Already, on the heights of Montmartre, is a digging and delving; too like a scarping and trenching. The effluence of Paris is arrested Versailles-ward by a barrier at Sèvres Bridge. From the Queen's Mews, cannon stand pointed on the National Assembly Hall itself. The National Assembly has its very slumbers broken by the tramp of soldiery, swarming and defiling, endless, or seemingly endless, all round those spaces, at dead of night, 'without drum music, without audible word of command'. What means it?"

The presence of large numbers of foreign troops added one more element to the volatile mixture – that is, French *patriotism* - and fed by popular antipathy towards the queen and her Austrian connection the fusion of revolutionary and patriotic sentiments was to become one of the potent political forces in the days that followed. On the 8th July Mirabeau intervened in the Assembly proceedings to say that all the roads and bridges around Paris had become military posts as if there were some great "preparation for war": "Why all these preparations? ..To maintain order, to contain the people?…Such precautions, instead of calming the people, will alarm them, and will agitate them." And prophetically: "What if the soldiers get electrified by their contact with the capital; what if they get interested in our political discussions, and, mixing with worried citizens, some soldiers become insubordinate, and resort to some impetuous actions; sedition will march with its head up. What would happen to the authors of these measures when the general conflagration shall be lit everywhere, when the drunken people launches itself into the excesses whose extreme I fear to think of…" Have they "..foreseen the consequences they entail for the safety of the throne? Have they studied in the history of all people's, how revolutions begin..?"[9] It is interesting to note that

Mirabeau for one well understood the difference between the kind of revolution in which he was playing such a prominent role and the violent overthrow of a government in which as he puts it, "sedition will march with its head up." Mirabeau proposed the formation of "une garde bourgoise" but on an amendment of de Biauzat this was reserved for 'another time'. Deputations were sent to the king objecting to the presence of the troops but all to no avail. But these protestations – for that is all they ever amounted to – were rapidly overtaken by what was happening in the capital ten miles away.

The broad outline of events from the 11th to the 16th July has been amply documented and only the main points need mentioned here. On the 12th news leaked out that on the previous day Necker, popular not least because he favoured food subsidies and control of the grain trade, was ordered out of the country and a new conservative ministry formed under Breteuil with Marshal de Broglie as minister of war. Whether this was the first sign of the feared attack and the suppression of public protest hardly mattered for this is how it was interpreted in Paris. Wax busts of Necker and d'Orléans were paraded through the streets and led to a confrontation with cavalry from the Royal Allemand but the demonstrators were joined by a contingent of the Gardes Françaises who in a related incident also pushed back some troops of the Salis-Samade. It was at this point that Desmoulins and others called for arms and the search began for these and also for stores of food. Following a similar outbreak in Lyons the customs barriers controlling the entry of provisions into Paris were burned down and the premises of armourers looted. On the same evening the Electors of Paris formed a municipal authority which decreed the formation of a militia forty-eight thousand strong and made up of middle-class citizens – we are not speaking here of a revolutionary army of the proletariat – a force "…substantial enough to perform its twin duties of facing down any further attempt at military repression and containing and, if necessary, punishing unlawful violence."[10] The Paris militia was intended to be only defensive for professional soldiers on both sides, Lafayette on the one and Besenval on the other, knew well enough that as things stood on that day an ill-prepared and poorly equipped body of this kind would be no match for experienced troops armed with cannon and grapeshot. What worried de Broglie was the dangerous example set by some members of the Gardes Françaises which if followed by regiments composed largely of French nationals might prove, as Mirabeau had prophesied, catastrophic.

In Versailles Lafayette proposed that the main responsibility for the disorders in Paris and the provinces rested with Breteuil and his ministers whose provocative policies had brought the explosive situation about. As in the Réveillon and some other incidents it was rumoured that dark forces were again at work, this time with the aim of inflaming the situation to the point where a full-scale military assault could be launched under the pretext of restoring public order. And then there was the criminal element, referred to by Bailly and others as "brigands" masquerading as patriots and bent upon exploiting the situation for their own nefarious purposes (*Memoirs*, vol.1: 337). Once again the Assembly re-affirmed the inviolability of its Deputies and declared that it would not abandon its earlier decrees "...notably those of the 17th, 20th and 23rd of last June"[11]. During the search for arms further evidence of advance military preparations came to light when it was discovered that a store of gunpowder had been moved from the arsenal at the Hôtel des Invalides to a barge on the Seine and a larger amount to the Bastille prison whose defences had been strengthened by a unit of the Salis-Samade. Attention thus turned to the Bastille, but it was not the Paris militia that set out on the morning of the 14th of July and even for the small number that did the aim was not the abolition of the monarchy or the deposition of the king. In the popular literature the emphasis given to this day tends to obscure the significance of the constitutional changes in June and also feeds into that bizarre and theatrical kind of romanticism which imagines that a popular revolution cannot happen without rivers of blood and lots of very loud noises. Nor was the 14th July the great revolt of the Paris citizenry it is so often presented as being for whilst it is true that the Bastille was seen as a symbol of despotism the number of those actively involved in bringing about its surrender was exceedingly small; less than a thousand citizens re-enforced in the afternoon by sixty soldiers of the Gardes Françaises does not count as a mass uprising in a city with an adult population of over half a million[12]. Even so, the bravery shown on that day together with the part played by the Gardes Françaises and the increasingly questionable loyalty of the regiments was enough to convince de Broglie to back down and on his advice the king announced the withdrawal of troops from the centre of Paris and the recall of Necker. On the 15th Lafayette was appointed commander of the

Paris militia, now re-constituted as the National Guard, and Bailly as Mayor of the city.

Something must also be said about the summary executions and barbaric treatment of de Launay the governor of the Bastille, Flessselles the chief magistrate of Paris, Bertier de Sauvigny the intendant of the city and his father-in-law and one-time member of Breteuil's ministry, Foulon. Speaking of The Terror in 1793/4 Schama (1989:447) writes: "The terror was merely 1789 with a higher body count. From the first year it was apparent that violence was not just an unfortunate side effect from which enlightened Patriots could selectively avert their eyes; it was the Revolution's source of collective energy. It was what made the Revolution revolutionary." This flamboyant remark, worthy of Burke himself, contradicts Schama's own analysis that the assumption of sovereignty by the National Assembly on the 20th of June was not accompanied by any violence on the part of that body – there were no executions and no heads on pikes. Like Schama, Hibbert (1982: 63) also uses the word 'revolution' equivocally but he at least provides a defensible historical summary of developments up to 27th June: "The first stage of the Revolution was over and had been achieved without bloodshed." None of the barbarism which broke out on the 14th July was ordered or sanctioned by the Assembly and if one includes among the 'enlightened patriots' people like Bailly it is not true to say that they averted their eyes. Carlisle for example records the efforts of Bailly and the municipality to bring Foulon to a properly constituted trial[13] and although the treatment meted out by the furious crowd was blithely dismissed by some like Barnave –

"Is this blood then so pure that one should so regret to spill it?" – but it was also criticised by many others and even Marat maintained that those involved were merely imitating the brutality of their masters. In answer to Burke's *Reflections* Paine makes the same point when he refers to the example set by the ruling classes of Europe as "government by terror" and so far as this kind of behaviour is concerned he had no more sympathy for the mobility than he had for the nobility: "There is in all European countries, a large class of people of that description which in England is called the '*mob*'. Of this class were those that committed the burnings and devastations in London in 1780, and of this class were those who carried the heads upon spikes in Paris. Foulon and Berthier were taken up in the country, and sent to Paris, to undergo their examination at the Hotel de Ville; for the National Assembly, immediately on the new ministry coming into office, passed a decree, which they communicated to the King and the Cabinet, that they (the National Assembly) would hold the ministry, of which Foulon was one, responsible for the measures they were advising and pursuing; but the mob, incensed at the appearance of Foulon and Berthier, tore them from their conductors before they were carried to the Hotel de Ville, and executed them on the spot. Why then does Mr Burke charge outrages of this kind on a whole people?...These outrages were not the effect of the principles of the Revolution, but of the degraded mind that existed before the Revolution, and which the Revolution is calculated to reform...It is to the honour of the National Assembly, and the city of Paris, that during such a tremendous scene of arms and confusion, beyond the control of all authority, they have been able, by the influence of example and exhortation, to restrain so much." (1985:57/9).

Looking back at the sequence of events from 17th June to 16th July some important conclusions can be drawn. Firstly, if it is historically correct to speak as Doyle (2002: 421) himself does of "...the seizure of sovereignty by the representatives of the nation in June 1789, confirmed by the popular action of mid-July" then one is bound to conclude that the first and critical political development was not the popular action of mid-July but the one it served to confirm. In his popular account of The French Revolution (2001: 40) Doyle is even more emphatic on the constitutional importance of the 17th June: "Once again at Sieyè's instigation, on June 17th it chose an obvious but uncompromising title: the National Assembly. Immediately afterwards it decreed the cancellation and then re-authorization of all taxes. The implication was clear. The Assembly had seized sovereign power in the name of the French nation. It was the founding act of the French Revolution. If the Nation was sovereign, the king no longer was." Although Grab (1989:46) seems to be inspired by the "Jacobino-Marxist Vulgate" he says the same when speaking of the 17th June: "This decision, which transferred sovereignty from the king to the nation, was revolutionary, for it replaced the privileged order with a modern system of representation founded on legal equality." Secondly, if the citizens of St. Antoine were correct in regarding themselves as defenders of the revolution and saviours of the National Assembly then obviously in their view some kind of revolution had already taken place. Thirdly, the 'popular action' of mid-July, in which the formation of the Paris militia and the municipal authority should also be included, was essentially defensive in conception and largely so in prosecution. And this brings one back to the period between the 5th May and the 20th of June and Kant's much-derided interpretation of the constitutional change during that time.

Kant had received regular news from France including direct reports from correspondents like J.B.Jachmann who was in Paris during the celebrations marking the first anniversary of 14th July and who gives a revealing account of the degenerating condition of proceedings in the Constituent Assembly. Thus there is no reason to suppose that when the *Rechtslehre* was written eight years later Kant did not know exactly what had happened in France, especially in the critical period between May and June of 1789. Yet in his interpretation of Kant's remarks in the *Rechtslehre* Williams (1983:211/12) writes: "In Kant's view, therefore, it was not so much the Estates General which wrested authority from the King, as the King himself who resigned from his constitutional post as sovereign. This was, he suggests, a voluntary transfer of power which fell within the range of what he regarded as permissible reforms. The transfer of power from the Crown to the people was constitutional and legitimate because it was a change which was initiated by the sovereign himself. This argument is far from sound. It may well be that the French King played into the hands of the Third Estate by requesting them to vote him increased funds, but it is misleading to suggest that by doing this the King voluntarily gave up his authority as sovereign. The truth of the matter was that he was forced to give up his absolute authority by the violent events going on around him. Here Kant sets himself an impossible task in trying to detach the constitutional changes that took place in France from the political and social turmoil surrounding them."

This interpretation is both inaccurate and highly idiosyncratic. Kant does not say that the king 'resigned'; he does not suggest a 'voluntary transfer of power'; and he does not say that this was 'initiated by the sovereign himself'. And if it was not Kant's view that the Estates General had wrested sovereign authority from the king then all the events before and after the Séance Royale of 23rd June would be inexplicable not only to him but to other contemporary observers like Arthur Young. The only explicit addition required to make Kant's remark in the *Rechtslehre* fully consistent with his understanding of Erhard's concept of *eine Revolution des Volks* is that this wresting of sovereign authority was not brought about by an attempt to violently overthrow the existing monarchical constitution. Furthermore, if there is no evidence to suggest that the political turmoil involved in this transfer of sovereignty was part of a violent assault on the monarchy, nor is there any to suggest that the social turmoil surrounding it was itself motivated by this particular aim.

When Kant writes of a "serious error of judgement" by Louis XVIth he could not mean that merely convening the Estates-General would necessarily lead to the loss of absolute power for on the last occasion this body had met in 1614 there was no such outcome. Presumably Kant means that in the greatly changed economic and social circumstances of 1789 this was not a wise course of action, a fateful decision that appears to be based on the advice of Necker. But powerful countervailing influences also had their effect and there is a much truth in Carlisle's observation that the king "...means well, had he any fixed meaning". Again presumably, Kant thought that had the king the determination to do so he might have forced through the required reforms and provided the policies he might have pursued did not conflict with the rights of the citizen he would be have been justly entitled to do so. This would have involved a direct confrontation with the first two Orders but had the king applied himself to this task rather than to hunting, making locks and eating pies things might well have taken a very different course.

So was there a revolution in France in 1789? If by 'revolution' one means the forcible overthrow of the constitution that existed before 20th June then the historical evidence does not support the view that such an event ever took place. But if one means (as Erhard puts it) "a radical change in the constitution of a state" and one brought about without the use or threat of armed force then the transformation of an absolute into a constitutional monarchy surely falls into this category. This conclusion supports Kant's contention that the "event of our times" in the early months of 1789 is more properly described as *eine Revolution des Volks* rather than *eine Revolution*. In his terminology it also follows that the attempt to reverse this change by force of arms is to be regarded as a failed attempt at *eine Revolution* directed against a successful *Revolution des Volks*.

Notes to Part II

1. Mason, L. and Rizzo, T. *The French Revolution. A Document Collection.* pp. 52/3.

2. Furet, F. *The French Revolution, 1770-1814.* pp. 4/5

3. Mason, L. and Rizzo, T. pp.60/61.

4. *Travels in France*, 4.26

5. Mason, L. and Rizzo, T. pp. 62/65

6. *ibid.* p. 65

7. *Travels in France*, 4.32

8. Hibbert, C. *The French Revolution.* p.62.

9. Bailly, *Memoirs* vol.1 pp.293/5. Bailly expresses surprise at these remarks since it seemed to him that Mirabeau had some definite foreknowledge of what might happen. It is known that Mirabeau remained in close contact with the king and was in fact a paid secret adviser (Doyle, 2002:146). It might be that questions about the reliability of the regiments had been seriously discussed in the ministry and that Mirabeau had learned of this from the king. By bringing the issue out into the open, especially to the ears of the

10. Schama, *Citizens*, p.387

11. Bailly, *Memoirs*, vol. 1, p.342

12. Fierro (1998) estimates the population of Paris in 1789 as 650,000. For the Bastille Schama gives a figure of nine hundred citizens and Hibbert (1982: 82) the following estimates of the numbers involved: "…eighty-three of the assailants were killed, fifteen died from wounds, and seventy-three were wounded. Most of them were artisans from the Faubourg Saint-Antoine who had been born outside Paris where they had come to find work. Of those who survived the assault 954 were awarded the title of *Vainqueur de la Bastille* the following June." The defence was made up of eighty-two army pensioners reinforced by thirty-two soldiers from the Salis-Samade and so the defenders were outnumbered by about ten to one. It is not clear why Besenval did not intervene even though he had sufficient troops nearby and plenty of time to deploy them. It is interesting to note that in his *Chronology* of the city Fierro, who in 1998 was Chief Librarian of the Historical Library of the City of Paris, states for the year 1789: "The fall of the Bastille symbolizes the start of the Revolution." So much for history. When de Launay surrendered late in the afternoon only seven prisoners were found inside: "Four were forgers who had been transferred there from some other, overcrowded prison; one was a mentally unbalanced Irishman who, believing himself

alternately Julius Caesar and God, was supposed to be a spy; the sixth, also deranged, was suspected of being involved in an attempt to assassinate the King; the last was the Comte de Salage whose family had arranged for him to be committed by a *lettre de cachet* for incest." (Hibbert, p.72).

13. With the *Histoire Parlementaire* as his main source Carlyle describes the fate of Foulon: "Sooty Saint-Antoine, and every street, musters its crowd as he passes; - the Hall of the Hôtel-de-Ville, the Place de Grève itself, will scarcely hold his escort and him. Foulon must not only be judged righteously, but judged there where he stands, without any delay. Appoint seven judges, ye Municipals, or seventy-and seven; name them yourselves, or we will name them: but judge him! Electoral rhetoric, eloquence of Mayor Bailly, is wasted, for hours, explaining the beauty of the Law's delay. Delay and still delay! Behold O Mayor of the People, the morning has worn itself into noon: and he is still unjudged! - Lafayette, pressingly sent for, arrives: gives voice: This Foulon, a known man, is guilty almost beyond doubt; but may he not have accomplices? Ought not the truth to be cunningly pumped out of him, - in the Abbaye prison? It is a new light! Sansculottism claps hands; - at which handclapping Foulon (in his fainness, as his Destiny would have it) also claps. See! They understand one another!" cries dark Sansculottism, blazing into fury of suspicion. – "Friends," said 'a person in good clothes,' stepping forward, "what is the use of judging this man? Has he not been judged these thirty years?" With wild yells, Sansculottism clutches him, in its hundred hands: he is whirled across the Place de Grève, to the '*Lanterne*,'

Lamp-iron which there is at the corner of the *Rue de la Vannerie*; pleading bitterly for life, – to the deaf winds. Only with the third rope (for two ropes broke, and the quavering voice still pleaded,) can he be so much as got hanged! His Body is dragged through the streets; his Head goes aloft on a pike, the mouth filled with grass; amid sounds as of Tophet, from a grass-eating people."

CONCLUSION

Amongst other requirements Kant's political strategy involves the non-violent evolution towards a republican constitution together with a forceful defence of inalienable rights and one may wonder why this standpoint has not been presented before in the secondary literature. The view taken here is that this is not due to confusions and inconsistencies in Kant's ethical works but to features of his philosophical method and style of presentation that often go unappreciated. Firstly, there is the difficulty arising from his attempt to develop consistency throughout the Critical Philosophy, an approach based on his belief that there can be only one *pure* reason which differs solely in its sphere of application. Whether or not Kant succeeds in this enterprise has long been disputed but his attempt to do so means that it is not possible to approach any of his works in a piecemeal fashion or in isolation from the rest. Thus in his practical philosophy the *Critique of Practical Reason* presupposes the *Groundwork of the Metaphysics of Morals* and from a philosophical point of view at least this itself requires familiarity with the phenomenal/noumenal distinction and the nature of synthetic *a priori* practical propositions. This in turn leads to the epistemology of the *Critique of Pure Reason* and in the absence of an understanding of this neither part of *The Metaphysics of Morals* will make much sense. And as we have seen, Kant's political philosophy arises directly from his ethical principles and any confusion about the latter will inevitably be reflected in the former. But secondly, Kant has a pronounced tendency to develop a concept or principle, perhaps give an example or two of its application and then expect the reader to work the rest out for himself. There are many examples of this approach in his ethical works and is often the source of so many complaints about a lack of coherence. The reader is entitled to expect clear definitions of concepts and principles but anyone who wants to be spoon-fed rather than carefully attending to what is being said and exercising their own powers of reason will not get far with Kant.

Where his views on revolution are concerned there is an additional problem. Throughout his published works and correspondence on this subject Kant demonstrates an extreme caution – some might say timidity - in exactly what he says and how he says it and it should be remembered that from 1789 Prussia and France were in a permanent state of hostility which broke out into war in 1792 and at various times thereafter. Kant's cautious approach was also adopted by correspondents of his in Berlin and elsewhere, as Kiesewetter indicates in a letter to Kant in June 1793: "I believe that there are many interesting things to be said about the rationality of the basic principles on which the French Republic bases itself, if only it were prudent to write about such things..." [580]. For the same reason Kant declined an invitation from Spener to re-issue the *Universal History* and relate it to contemporary events in France: "I cannot agree to the proposal to publish a new, separate edition in the *Berliner Monatsschrift*, "Idea for a Universal History from a Cosmopolitan Point of View", least of all with addenda directed at current affairs. If the powerful of this world are in a drunken fit, be it the result of the breath of some god or emanations from a damped fire, then one must strongly advise a pygmy who values his skin to stay out of their fight, even if the encouragement to get mixed up in it should come in a most gentle and respectful entreaty. The main reason is that they would not listen to him at all, while those scandalmongers who do hear him would misinterpret what he says." [417]. It is partly due to this reluctance that Biester and many others were unsure of Kant's attitude towards the events in France until *Theory and Practice* was published in 1793. But it is also evident that Kant simply refused to be swept along by the tide of romanticism which accompanied 1789 or by the current of conservative reaction against it and was determined to develop a view consistent with the ethical principles he had formulated in 1784/5. To declare against revolution in the France of 1793 might well be the last words one would ever speak and this was obviously not the case in Prussia at that time but it is one thing for someone like Rehberg to oppose *eine Revolution* from the standpoint of 'the powers that be' and quite another to defend at the same time the inviolable rights of Man.

It seems that Kant's approach was to confine his public statements to what he felt obliged to say but otherwise to keep strictly within the laws of the Prussian state and not to provide it with any excuses to further censor his works. As a result his abbreviated references to revolution, especially where France is concerned, can sometimes make his position difficult to discern and his arguments not so easy to follow. But none of this will prove insurmountable to the serious student and as argued here Kant does have a consistent and defensible view of revolution so long as one takes the trouble to identify the relevant concepts and trace their various interconnections. And on this architectonic point one can do no better than cite his forthright response to the diffident critics of his own day, a remark that the modern neo-kantian would do well to ponder deeply before launching into yet another incoherent account of his practical philosophy:

"When we have to study a particular faculty of the human mind in its sources, its content, and its limits; then from the nature of human knowledge we must begin with its parts, with an accurate and complete exposition of them; complete, namely, so far as is possible in the present state of our knowledge of its elements. But there is another thing to be attended to which is of a more philosophical and architectonic character, namely to grasp correctly the idea of the whole, and from thence to get a view of all those parts as mutually related by the aid of pure reason, and by means of their derivation from the concept of the whole. This is only possible through the most intimate acquaintance with the system; and those who find the first enquiry too troublesome, and do not think it worth their while to attain such an acquaintance, cannot reach the second stage, namely, the general view, which is a synthetical return to that which had previously been given analytically. It is no wonder then if they find inconsistencies everywhere, although the gaps which these indicate are not in the system itself, but in their own incoherent train of thought." [V: 10]

BIBLIOGRAPHY

Beck, L.W. Introduction to *Kant on History*. Bobbs-Merrill: Indianapolis, 1957.

Beck, L.W. Kant and the Right of Revolution. *Journal of the History of Ideas*. Vol.32, No.3 (July-Sept., 1971) pp.411-422.

Carlyle, T. *The French Revolution. A History*. Vol. I. Collins: London, 1837.

Cobban, A. *The Myth of the French Revolution*. London: H.K.Lewis, 1955.

Doyle, W. *The Oxford History of the French Revolution*. 2nd ed. Oxford: OUP, 2002.

Doyle, W. *The French Revolution. A Very Short Introduction*. Oxford. OUP, 2001.

Erhard, J.B. *Über das Recht des Volks zu einer Revolution und andere Schriften*. Herausgegeben von Hellmut G. Haasis. Carl Hanser Verlag: Munich, 1970.

Fierro, A. *Historical Dictionary of Paris*. Trans. Woronoff, J. Scarecrow Press: Lanham, Md., & London, 1998.

Flikschuh, K. Reason, Right, and Revolution: Kant and Locke. *Philosophy & Public Affairs*. Vol.36, Issue 4, 2008, pp. 375-404.

Furet, F. *The French Revolution, 1770-1814*. Blackwell: Oxford, 1992.

Geiger, I. What is the Use of the Universal Law Formula of the Categorical Imperative? *British Journal for the History of Philosophy.* 18 (2) 2010, 271-95

Gooch, P. *Germany and the French Revolution* (1920). 2nd Impression. Longmans: London, 1927.

Grab, W. *The French Revolution.* Bracken Books: London, 1989.

Herman, B. *The Practice of Moral Judgement:* Harvard University Press, Cambridge, Mass., 1993.

Hettner, H. *Geschichte der Deutschen Literatur im XVIII. Jahhundert.* Paul List Verlag: Leipzig, 1928.

Hibbert, C. *The French Revolution.* Penguin Books: London, 1982.

Hill, Thomas E. *Respect, Pluralism and Justice:* O.U.P, Oxford, 2000.

Hill, Thomas E. Questions About Kant's Opposition to Revolution. The Journal of Value Enquiry. Vol.36 (2002), nos. 2-3, pp. 283-298.

Kant, I. *Conflict of the Faculties.* Trans. Gregor, M.J. University of Nebraska Press: Lincoln, 1979.

Kant, I. *Critique of Practical Reason.* Trans. Gregor, M.J. C.U.P: Cambridge, 1997.

Kant, I. *The Metaphysics of Morals.* Trans. Gregor, M.J. C.U.P: Cambridge, 1996.

Kant, I. *Anthropology from a Pragmatic Point of View*. Trans. Gregor, M.J. Martinus Nijhoff: The Hague, 1974.

Kant, I. *Idea for a Universal History from a Cosmopolitan Point of View*. In Kant. Political Writings. C.U.P: Cambridge, 1991.

Kant, I. *An Answer to the Question: What is Enlightenment?* In Reiss, *op.cit.*

Kant, I. *On the Common Saying: 'This May be True in Theory, but it Does Not Apply in Practice'*. In Reiss, *op.cit.*

Kant, I. *Perpetual Peace: A Philosophical Sketch*. In Reiss, *op.cit.*

Kant, I. *Review of Hufeland's Essay on the Principles of Natural Right*. In Immanuel Kant, Practical Philosophy. C.U.P, Cambridge, 1996.

Kant, I. *Religion within the Limits of Reason Alone*. Trans. Greene, T.M. and Hudson, H.H. Harper Torchbooks: New York, 1960.

Kant, I. *Religion within the Boundaries of Mere Reason*. Ed. Wood, A and Giovanni, G. di., C.U.P: Cambridge, 1998.

Kant, I. *Groundwork of the Metaphysics of Morals*. C.U.P: Cambridge, 1997.

Kant, I. *Philosophical Correspondence, 1759-99*. Ed. and Trans. Arnulf Zweig. University of Chicago Press: Chicago, 1967.

Kant, I. *Correspondence*. Ed. and Trans. Arnulf Zweig. C.U.P: Cambridge, 1999.

Korsgaard, C. *Creating the Kingdom of Ends*. C.U.P: Cambridge, 1996.

Korsgaard, C. *The Constitution of Agency*. O.U.P: Oxford, 2008.

Ladd, J. *Immanuel Kant. Metaphysical Elements of Justice*. 2nd ed. Hackett: Indianapolis, 1999.

MacIntyre, A. *After Virtue*. 2nd ed. Duckworth: London, 1990.

Mason, L. and Rizzo, T. *The French Revolution. A Document Collection*. Wadsworth: Boston, 1999.

Millgram, E. Does the Categorical Imperative Give Rise to a Contradiction in the Will? *The Philosophical Review*, Vol. 112, No. 4, 525-560 (October 2003).

Nicholson, P. Kant on the Duty Never to Resist the Sovereign. *Ethics*, Vol.86, No.3 (April 1976) pp.214-230.

Paine, T. *Rights of Man*. Penguin American Library 1984, New York. Penguin Classics: Harmondsworth, 1985.

Rehberg, A.W. *Über das Verhaltnis der Theorie zur Praxis* (1793), in *Über Theorie und Praxis*, ed. Dieter Henrich. Suhrkamp: Frankfurt, 1967.

Reiss, H. *Kant. Political Writings*. 2nd enlarged ed. C.U.P: Cambridge, 1991.

Rosen, A.D. *Kant's Theory of Justice*. Cornell University Press: Ithaca, 1993.

Schama, S. *Citizens. A Chronicle of the French Revolution*. Alfred A. Knopf: New York, 1989.

Schossberger, C. *The Kingdom of Ends and the Fourth Example in the Groundwork II*. Akten des X. Internationalen Kant-Kongresses, Band 3, 369-77, 2008.

Scurr, R. *Fatal Purity. Robespierre and the French Revolution*. Vintage Books: London, 2007.

Schwarz, W. The Ambiguities of 'Resistance': A Reply to Peter Nicholson. *Ethics*, Vol.87, No.3 (April 1977) pp.255-259.

Soboul, A. *A Short History of the French Revolution 1789-1799*. University of California Press: Berkeley, 1977.

Sullivan, R.J. *An Introduction to Kant's Ethics*. C.U.P: Cambridge, 1994.

Williams, H. *Kant's Political Philosophy*. St. Martin's Press: New York, 1983.

Williams, H. *Kant's Critique of Hobbes*. University of Wales Press: Cardiff, 2003.

Wood, A.W., *Kantian Ethics* (2008), Cambridge University Press.

Wood, A. W. *Kant's Ethical Thought*. C.U.P: Cambridge, 1999.

Yolton, J.S. *A Locke Miscellany: Locke Biography and Criticism for All.* Thoemmes, Bristol, 1990.

Young, A. *Travels in France During the Years 1787, 1788, 1789.* George Bell & Sons: London, 1906.

www.ingramcontent.com/pod-product-compliance
Lightning Source LLC
Chambersburg PA
CBHW071716040426
42446CB00011B/2091